CLASSIC NATURAL HISTORY PRINTS

BIRDS

ACKNOWLEDGMENTS

The author and publishers would like to thank the following for their help in the compilation of this book:
The National Museums of Scotland: David Heppell of the Department of Natural History; the Head of Library, Manjil V. Mathew and his staff. The National Library of Scotland, Edinburgh: the Superintendent of Reference Services. The Natural History Museum, London: the Head of Library Services, Rex Banks and his staff. The Linnean Society of London: the Council and Librarian, Gina Douglas. The Zoological Society of London: the Librarian, R.A. Fish. Ken Smith Photography (Edinburgh). The Glasgow Museum and Art Gallery, Kelvingrove: Fred Woodward of the Department of Natural History. Cavendish House, Carlisle: Una Dance, Robert Dance. Wheldon and Wesley Booksellers, Codicote: Howard Swann, Chairman and his staff.

They would also like to thank the following for their kind permission to photograph the original prints in their possession:
The Natural History Museum, London, for the plates appearing on pages 9, 17, 21, 23, 25, 37, 41, 43, 45, 59, 65, 75, 79, 85, 91, 93, 95, 97, 103, 105, 107, 113, 115, 119; The Linnean Society of London, for the plates appearing on pages 11, 13, 19, 29, 31, 33, 47, 49, 51, 53, 67, 69, 81, 83, 87, 89, 99, 109; The National Museums of Scotland, Edinburgh, for the plates appearing on pages 35, 39, 61, 63, 71, 73, 101, 111, 117, 121, 123; The Tryon Gallery, London, for the plates appearing on pages 125 and 127; The National Library of Scotland, Edinburgh for the plates appearing on pages 55 and 57; The Victoria & Albert Museum, London, for the plate appearing on page 15; Fred R. Woodward, Glasgow, for the plate appearing on page 27, and Una Dance, Carlisle, for the plate appearing on page 77.

Classic Natural History Prints, *Birds*
First published in Great Britain in 1990
by Collins & Brown Limited
Mercury House
195 Knightsbridge
London SW7 1RE

Created, designed and produced by Studio Editions Ltd
Princess House, 50 Eastcastle Street
London W1N 7AP, England

Printed and bound in Italy

ISBN 1 85585 065 6

CLASSIC NATURAL HISTORY PRINTS

BIRDS

MACROCERCUS ARACANGA.
Red and Yellow Macaw

S. PETER DANCE

COLLINS & BROWN

INTRODUCTION   5

LIST OF PLATES

INTRODUCTION

Birds are the brightest ornaments of the animal creation. Through the ages they have charmed us with their beauty, their behaviour and their song, and without their beguiling presence our world would be greatly impoverished. Fortunately they still exist in huge numbers and bewildering variety, scarcely any part of the globe being entirely without them.

The art of bird portraiture took much longer to mature than the art of flower painting. One reason for this was the importance of good illustrations to help physicians and others recognize plants of medical significance. Another was the fidgety nature of birds and their shyness. They do not willingly allow us near them, and unless they are captive may be admired only from a distance. Before the widespread use of binoculars the only way artists could get close enough to many of the birds they wanted to draw was to shoot them or have them shot on their behalf. As many of the finest bird illustrations were created from the study of preserved bird skins it follows that the use of increasingly efficient firearms was largely responsible for advancing the art of bird portraiture to the high point it reached towards the end of the nineteenth century – a sobering thought.

There are few convincing bird pictures in books published before the nineteenth century. With some notable exceptions the birds portrayed in them look lifeless, which, for the most part, they were. With monotonous regularity birds are shown perched stiffly on tree stumps or rustic-looking branches. Rarely are they shown in flight. As most of the birds depicted were dead, misshapen and often faded it is scarcely surprising that many of the early illustrations appear to us as caricatures.

The unnaturally wooden appearance of the birds in many of the early illustrations was also due to the artists' lack of curiosity and scientific interest in birds. It is noteworthy, too, that the artists' original drawings had to be engraved on wood, copper or steel by workers who often had little or no interest in the subjects represented in the drawings. Only when printing by lithography came into vogue was it possible for a bird artist to draw his subject on a smooth stone slab himself and have impressions of it transferred directly to paper. It was lithography, more than anything else, which gave life to bird art.

Before discussing the illustrators and their work it should be pointed out that the prints selected for this book include not only some of the finest ever published but also a few which display an inadequate understanding of birds. For one reason or another all are good examples of their kind and worthy of inclusion. An accurate representation of a bird may please us because it is accurate but, equally, an inaccurate one may delight us simply because it reveals the personality of the artist. Even the finest – perhaps especially the finest – bird pictures ever done are stamped with the personalities of their creators.

One of the first books to include hand coloured illustrations of birds was *A Natural History of Birds* by Eleazar Albin, published in three volumes between 1731 and 1738. It has the distinction of being the first comprehensive book about British birds, but it has little else to recommend it. Nearly all the birds are shown in profile, some are copied from illustrations in other books, different birds are given identical beaks, and the colours seem to have been applied randomly. But it was a beginning.

While Albin was busy concocting his curious pictures another Englishman, Mark Catesby, was engraving and colouring the plates for his large folio book, *The Natural History of Carolina, Florida and the Bahama Islands* (1731–43). About half of the 220 plates in this pioneering study of American natural history portray birds. Besides writing the text of his book Catesby taught himself the art of engraving so that he could engrave and subsequently colour all the plates himself, a monumental task.

Birds had an especial attraction for him. 'I painted them,' he said, 'while alive (except a very few) and gave them their gestures peculiar to every kind of Bird, and where it would admit of, I have adapted the Birds to those Plants on which they fed.'

Catesby taught the art of engraving to his friend George Edwards, a keen student of birds who, like Catesby, wanted to illustrate a book of his own but had insufficient money to employ engravers and colourists. In the book he eventually brought out, entitled *A Natural History of Uncommon Birds* (1743–51), the pupil emulated the teacher. Like Catesby, he maintained that he drew from living birds whenever possible, but admitted that he sometimes had to make do with dried and stuffed specimens. As he tried to show all the features of a species distinguishing it from other birds, he often sacrificed the opportunity to make a satisfying composition (although he was not averse to adding the occasional landscape background). Few nineteenth-century bird illustrators would have made this kind of sacrifice. The birds illustrated in his *Gleanings of Natural History* (1758–64), however, are rather more decorative.

Of course, British authors were not alone in publishing illustrations of birds during the first half of the eighteenth century. For instance, the four weighty volumes of Albert Seba's *Thesaurus* (1734–65) contain many engravings of birds and other natural objects, most of them having once formed a part of Seba's famous museum of curiosities at Amsterdam. Although most of the birds perch rather stiffly on spindly twigs the sheer size of the plates they decorate makes them seem more impressive than they are, especially in the few existing copies of the book which have been coloured by hand. It was to be many years before a book comparable in size and pictorial splendour to Seba's *Thesaurus* was published in Britain.

It is difficult to discuss any aspect of natural history in the eighteenth century without referring to George-Louis Leclerc, Comte de Buffon, the most influential philosopher–naturalist of his day. A haughty French aristocrat of ample means, Buffon conceived the idea of describing the entire natural world, its rocks, mountains, forests, seas, lakes and rivers, and all that lived on or in them. The first volume of his *Histoire Naturelle* appeared in 1749 and was followed by others in steady succession, each stylishly written and attractively illustrated with black and white engravings. He dealt with rocks and minerals, the human race, quadrupeds and some birds – and then died, his ambition unrealized, having published only 36 of a projected 50 volumes. Subsequently other naturalists attempted to finish what Buffon had begun and many more illustrated volumes were published, including several dealing with birds. A ten-volume luxury edition of the bird section, with highly coloured plates by François-Nicolas Martinet, began to appear before Buffon died; and other illustrated editions continued to appear until well into the nineteenth century. The influence of these different editions of Buffon's *Histoire* was long lasting and beneficial, the standard of bird portraiture improving significantly as a result.

That influence came too late for Xaverio Manetti, the Italian author of one of the most lavishly illustrated bird books of the eighteenth century, the *Ornithologia Methodice Digesta* (1767–76). His flamboyant, sometimes comical engravings of birds are almost unique, emulated only by the absurd, albeit delightful pastiches of them published by his contemporary Maddalena Bouchard. Birds are portrayed as though they walk with the aid of stilts, as though encased in knitted woollen bags, as though they have strayed out of Alice's Wonderland.

While Manetti was light-heartedly tackling his bird book,

Cornelis Nozeman was busy writing what was to become the finest book ever devoted to the birds of the Netherlands. Begun in 1770, his *Nederlandsche Vogelen* was not completed until 60 years later (by Martin Houttyn) and ultimately contained 250 splendid, folio-sized, hand coloured plates, each showing birds in their natural surroundings, and often with their nests and eggs. They outshine any plates illustrating the various editions of Buffon and, in an eighteenth-century context at least, may be considered far ahead of their time.

At the beginning of the nineteenth century, however, French bird books reigned supreme, the illustrations in several of them being well engraved, colour printed or coloured by hand, and sometimes heightened with gold. The traveller–naturalist François Levaillant, though not an artist himself, was the author of some of the most exquisitely illustrated bird books of all time. Apart from the plates reproduced in his *Histoire Naturelle des Oiseaux d'Afrique* (1796–1808), those which accompany Levaillant's various texts were taken from original drawings by Jacques Barraband, a superlatively talented artist who had been employed at the Gobelin tapestry works and at the Sèvres porcelain factory.

French book illustrators at that time were steeped in the traditional skills of miniature painting, so their work shows a mastery of minutely accurate drawing and a confident use of bright colours, including gold leaf. This mastery is seen in some of the illustrations to one of the most ambitious bird books of the period, the *Oiseaux Dorés ou à Reflets Métalliques* by Jean-Baptiste Audebert and Louis-Jean-Pierre Viellot, published in 1802. The plates show humming-birds, birds of paradise, and other birds endowed with gorgeous plumage. They were printed in colour and highlighted here and there with gold: a dozen copies of the book had the text printed in gold, and a single copy was printed entirely in gold on vellum. The resulting bird portraits were seldom true to nature, but they were very elegant, very French – and very expensive.

As these sumptuously illustrated books were produced exclusively by French artists, illustrators, writers and publishers it may be worth saying something about the tradition of miniature painting which inspired them, for they stand alone in the development of natural history illustration in general and of bird illustration in particular.

The story begins in the seventeenth century, when Gaston of Orleans, an enthusiastic naturalist and brother of Louis XIII, employed a talented miniaturist, Nicholas Robert, to portray the unusual and rare animals and plants in his garden. Robert's paintings, executed on sheets of parchment, are of an exceptionally high quality, combining a delicacy of touch and the use of brilliant but transparent colours with an awareness of the natural appearance and attitudes of animals. Robert died in 1685, but the collection he had started was augmented by pictures of animals and plants painted by other formidably gifted artists. Eventually there was a school of these artists whose job was to copy as exactly as possible the animals and plants which were being constantly studied at the National Museum in Paris. One of those artists was Pierre-Joseph Redouté, the famous painter of roses, which suggests that a very high artistic standard was expected.

Now it is time to tell the remarkable story of the world's most celebrated bird man, John James Audubon, a story inseparable from that of the unfortunate man he overshadowed, Alexander Wilson, who had emigrated from Paisley in Scotland towards the close of the eighteenth century and had enthusiastically taken up the study of birds in the North American wilderness. A novice in art and natural history, Wilson conceived the novel idea of writing and illustrating a luxurious book about the birds of North America: such a book had never been published before.

Wilson tramped wearily from town to city to outpost seeking subscribers to his grand design. Considering the very high cost of the subscription he pulled in a surprisingly large number of subscribers, 458 in all. One day in March 1810 he called at a store in Louisville, Kentucky, a tame parrot on his shoulder, portfolios of drawings under his arm, and asked the storekeeper if he could interest him in his project. The storekeeper was John James Audubon, son of a Frenchman and a Creole woman, and he could not afford the subscription – though he was too proud to admit it – for he and his partner were failing badly in business. But the conversation between Wilson and Audubon revealed that the latter had a large portfolio of his own bird drawings and this he opened in front of the Scotsman.

What Wilson then gazed upon, of course, were the first fruits of a talent which was ultimately to lift Audubon out of obscurity and ensure that his name would be revered for as long as men and women are captivated by wildlife and by highly original artistic interpretations of it. The storekeeper's drawings, though far inferior to those which would one day dazzle all who looked at them, were far better than Wilson's – and Wilson knew it. The difference between the two sets of drawings was the difference between the dead and the living: whereas Wilson had drawn all his birds stiffly and almost always in profile, Audubon's were supple and mobile; more than that, they were full of personality – Audubon's personality.

Although born in the West Indies, Audubon spent most of his youth in France where, among other things, he received some art instruction in the atelier of the famous Jacques-Louis David. When he was about 23 he spent a summer in France studying bird life with Alcide d'Orbigny, an excellent naturalist and the author of some magnificently illustrated works on natural history. That was the sum of Audubon's formal training in art and natural history. But drawing birds was his consuming passion and he stopped at nothing to increase his knowledge of them. He was an observant field naturalist and had extensive knowledge of bird behaviour, but to portray birds accurately he needed to observe them at close quarters. He became a crack shot and thought nothing of shooting large numbers of birds a day to ensure an adequate supply of study material: 'I call birds few, when I shoot less than one hundred per day' he is supposed to have said. Unlike those French artists who were trained at the National Museum in Paris Audubon learnt his craft in the open air. It was the American wilderness which turned him into an incomparable ornithologist and artist; that, and a certain amount of luck.

With the support of his faithful wife Lucy he managed to accumulate enough drawings to take to fashionable Philadelphia and seek out someone prepared to take the considerable risk of publishing them. In this he was less successful than Wilson, whose *American Ornithology* was published there. After two years Audubon had raised enough money to take his drawings to Edinburgh to look for publishers with more experience and enterprise than those in his own intellectually raw country. He found William Home Lizars, an excellent engraver and publisher, who agreed to engrave his drawings on 'double elephant folio', huge sheets on which it was possible to show even very large birds natural size. Publication of the largest bird book ever seen began in the early part of 1827 and was scheduled to be completed about fourteen years later, a truly colossal enterprise. The first results were greeted with acclaim and Audubon became a celebrity overnight.

Lizars unfortunately ran into trouble with his workforce and Audubon took off for London where he came across Robert Havell, a young and then obscure engraver, who agreed to take up where Lizars had left off. The results this time were even more pleasing. Havell had reproduced the original drawings by a process known as aquatint, a form of etching which gives tone effects of a transparent quality ideally suited for tinting with watercolours. Audubon was delighted and so were the subscribers to his book. He returned to America in 1829 to collect more birds and to see his wife but was back in London before the year was out. The problems associated with the publication of his great book were such that a lesser man would have capitulated and returned home, but he survived the vicissitudes which always seem to accompany this sort of project and saw it through to completion. Twelve years after it had been started, the eighty-seventh and final instalment was issued, Audubon returned home, and ornithology came of age.

The Birds of America did not give rise to a distinctive school of bird art: it is unique. The aquatint process, which was at least partly responsible for its visual impact, was too expensive to be widely used in other illustrated natural history books. Fortunately, a cheaper alternative was at hand: lithography.

Lithography began to come into general use at about the same time as Audubon's great book was being brought out. It proved to be admirably suited to the illustration of birds and other creatures. And that is how we come to a most unlikely fellow in the development of bird art: Edward Lear. He is much better known as the man who wrote nonsense rhymes and illustrated them with amusing line drawings, but he was first a very accomplished artist whose illustrations of birds and other animals are of a very high standard. In about 1828 he began to earn a living by drawing birds. In 1830 he obtained permission to draw the parrots in the Zoological Gardens in London, and in 1832, shortly before his twentieth birthday, the final instalment of his *Illustrations of the Family of Psittacidae, or Parrots* was published.

One of the men who engaged Lear's services was John Gould, about whom there is much to tell, for his contribution to the illustrated literature of birds is unequalled. Like Audubon, he became known as 'The Bird Man'. Unlike Audubon, he was a good businessman. Considering his boundless ambition and the amount of work he took on, he needed to be. The possibilities of lithography having become apparent to him at about the same time as they had to Lear he persuaded his wife Elizabeth to learn how to draw birds on the stone. She learnt quickly. At the first meeting of the British Association for the Advancement of Science, held at York in 1831, delegates were able to compare Audubon's drawings of American birds with those of birds from the Himalayas by Elizabeth Gould, a comparison undoubtedly to Audubon's advantage and giving little indication of the wonderful things to come from the Gould stable.

Soon a large work, *The Birds of Europe*, was under way. Of necessity Gould, accompanied by his wife and Edward Lear, travelled in Europe to study birds in zoos and museums. Then they got down to the work proper, the book appearing between 1832 and 1837 in five folio volumes and containing 449 magnificent hand coloured plates. Of these plates the best by far are those done by the bespectacled Lear – he was particularly good at owls, to which birds he considered he bore some resemblance – even though some of them are attributed on the plates to 'J. & E. Gould'. The production of Gould's folios illustrating birds now began in earnest and soon he was presiding over a factory of artists and colourists. A monograph on toucans was speedily followed by a book about birds from various parts of the globe and a monograph of the trogons. There followed a multi-volume book on Australian birds (he went to Australia with Elizabeth to do the groundwork for this), and also a monograph on the partridges of America.

But Gould still had much to achieve, including his acknowledged masterpiece, *A Monograph of the Trochilidae, or Family of Humming-birds*, and multi-volume books on the birds of Asia, Great Britain, New Guinea – birds of everywhere, it seemed – all of them gorgeous to look at and wonderful to own, if you had the money.

Gould's ambition required much more than a dutiful wife could provide and he sought out other artists whose talents could be moulded to his purpose. Henry Constantine Richter joined him in 1841 and William Hart was added to his team ten years later. Richter worked up Gould's rough sketches into finished watercolours from which lithographs were prepared. Hart's first job was to prepare patterns for the great five-volume monograph of the humming-birds and to touch in the metallic parts of these jewel-like creatures with gold when the patterns were transformed into lithographs; he soon graduated to more responsible work. Gould could not have completed a tenth part of his ambitious enterprises without the assistance of Richter and Hart.

But the German artist Joseph Wolf was the feather Gould most wanted in his cap. Wolf, possibly the finest wildlife artist of the nineteenth century and with few equals in the twentieth, was a master of dramatic composition and unrivalled as an illustrator of predatory birds. Gould admired his work greatly and knew him well, but Wolf did not like the kind of routine work Gould would have expected of him, preferring to accept more interesting commissions. Nevertheless he painted 80 or more watercolour studies for Gould, including many reproduced in *The Birds of Great Britain*. Of all the folio bird plates published by Gould the most vivid, the most dramatic and the most true are those from Wolf's original watercolours.

What Wolf would not do for Gould he was prepared to do for Daniel Giraud Elliot, a wealthy American from Chicago with an inordinate fondess of birds and a burning desire to emulate Gould's achievements in the production of sumptuously illustrated folios illustrating and describing them. Wolf painted fine watercolours of birds of paradise, pheasants and other magnificent birds for Elliot, which were published as outstanding hand coloured lithographs. The lithographs of the pheasants were executed by John Gerrard Keulemans, a Dutchman who had moved to London in 1869 to take up a professional career as a bird artist.

Keulemans may have drawn and lithographed more bird pictures than anyone else in the nineteenth century, but he seems to have worked for almost everyone except Gould. His bird pictures are often fine, occasionally exquisite, always adequate, but they lack the vitality and imagination of Wolf's. His work is often reproduced but he may rightly be labelled 'the honest journeyman of bird art', the artist who could reconstruct the probable appearance of a bird from its lifeless skin time after time after time.

By the end of the nineteenth century the outdoor approach to bird art began to prevail. As Richter, Hart, Wolf and Keulemans vacated the stage, so Thorburn, Lodge and Frohawk stepped on to it. Wolf had sometimes been guilty of introducing a Victorian sentimentality into his compositions. It was time for a more vital, more objective realism to take over. In Britain, the work of the Scottish wildlife artist Archibald Thorburn came into favour. He contributed many excellent plates to Lord Lilford's *Coloured Figures of the Birds of the British Islands* (1885–98) and went on to write and illustrate several impressive colour-plate books about British birds published under his own name. He also produced a number of high-quality prints of birds in signed, limited editions.

Thorburn's contemporary and rival, George Lodge, is judged the superior artist of the two by some competent people. This judgment may be sound if based on an inspection of their original paintings, Lodge's birds being well observed and placed in very attractive and naturalistic settings; but sometimes they lose their sparkle and freshness in printed reproductions, which tend to be smaller than the originals. Many of Lodge's finest bird paintings are contained in D. A. Bannerman's *Birds of the British Isles* (1953).

The illustrations in these and other publications show that if bird art came of age with the work of John James Audubon in North America, it came to life with the work of artists based in Europe. The artistic tradition which nurtured all of them was European, but it was North America which provided the vital impetus from which they all benefited. The very different influences of the Old World and the New combined to advance and enrich the art of bird portraiture. Those influences will operate on bird artists for as long as there are birds to portray.

Hoopoe

Hoop or Hoopoe Hen (now Hoopoe, *Upupa epops*). Hand coloured etching, pl. 42 from Vol. 2 of Eleazar Albin's *A Natural History of Birds, with Copper Plates, Curiously Engraven from Life*, 1731–38. Size of plate 9¾″ × 8″.

Apart from showing us a characteristic pose of the Hoopoe the plate reproduced here is interesting because it was published in the earliest illustrated book about British birds, was engraved by the author after one of his own drawings, and was issued hand coloured (a rare circumstance in Albin's day). The stiff pose and contrived perch were to be echoed in a majority of eighteenth-century bird illustrations published in Europe and North America. We may be certain that Albin's original drawing was taken from a stuffed specimen of the bird because he tells us he received it from a Mr Starkey Mayor who had shot it in his garden at Woodford, Epping Forest. It was unusual then for birds to be drawn from living examples.

The bird's strange English name is said to be derived from its distinctive call, *up up*; but the bird is called 'Huppe' in French which employs the same word to denote a bird's crest. Certainly the crest is the Hoopoe's most distinctive feature and has assured it a place in the folklore and legends of Europe, Africa, Arabia, India and Malaysia. It is also the feature which makes Albin's illustration so arresting, in spite of the bird's stiff pose.

The Cock Hoopoe.

Common Cardinal

RED BIRD, (now Common Cardinal, *Cardinalis cardinalis*). Hand coloured engraving by Mark Catesby, pl. 38 from Vol. 1 of his *The Natural History of Carolina, Florida and the Bahama Islands*, 1731–43. Size of plate 13¾″ × 10¼″.

Few visitors to the United States of America fail to be impressed by their first sight of the Cardinal as it flits among the trees or hops about on suburban lawns. So familiar and so common that it is often taken for granted by residents, the Cardinal is the best known – though not necessarily the most musical – of the New World songbirds, immediately recognizable by its clear, ringing whistle. For this reason it was once a popular cage bird. It is often looked upon as the only all-red bird in North America, though the same view is taken of the Summer Tanager, once known as the Summer Red Bird. Neither bird can rightly claim to be all red. The male Cardinal has a black throat and its eyes are linked by a black band; the male Summer Tanager has a yellow bill.

This is a very early illustration of the Cardinal and does less than justice to the bird, but since Catesby was a pioneer of North American natural history who taught himself how to engrave his own illustrations he may be forgiven a little stiffness in his birds. Pioneering is very difficult: criticizing is ridiculously easy.

Nux juglans Virginiana alba &c.
The Hiccory Tree.

The Pig-nut.

Coccothraustes ruber.
The red Bird.

Pelican

PELICAN, (presumably the White Pelican, *Pelecanus onocrotalus*). Hand coloured engraving by George Edwards, pl. 92 from Part 2 of his *A Natural History of Uncommon Birds*, 1743–51. Size of plate 11″ × 8″.

As five of the six living species of Pelicans are white with black wingtips it is not certain which of them was a model for this plate, but it was probably the White Pelican, which breeds in southern Europe, Africa, north-west India and western Asia. A large bird, its short legs and webbed feet make it clumsy on land, but its nine-foot wingspan helps it to fly with consummate ease; it is also a very good swimmer.

Grotesque in some ways, comical in others, the White Pelican and its close relatives have caused several curious notions. One of these says that the Pelican lives on the milk of the crocodile and so chooses to follow that animal. Another says that the Pelican sleeps with its bill held upright to protect itself from hawks. Yet another, embodied in a famous limerick, says that it can 'hold in its beak enough food for a week', a belief surely promoted by the knowledge that its capacious pouch, which can hold almost three gallons of water, is often filled to bursting with fish which it scoops up into it from the sea.

Most outlandish of all was the belief, widely circulated during the Middle Ages, that the female can tear open her breast to feed the nestlings with her own blood. Could the bright red tip of the Pelican's beak, seen against the white breast, have been mistaken for a spot of blood? Perhaps not. But there is a good reason for the many extraordinary things that have been said about the Pelican: it is an extraordinary bird.

G. Edwards. 1746.

92

Dodo

DODO [AND GUINEY PIG], *(Raphus cucullatus)*. Hand coloured engraving by George Edwards, pl. 294 from his *Gleanings of Natural History*, 1758–64. Size of plate 9¼″ × 7¼″.

The Dodo is one of the few birds that existed until modern times whose appearance is known only from pictures by artists who may have seen it alive; not one complete example of it has been preserved. Long before George Edwards published this evocative picture, the flightless Dodo had been exterminated in its native island of Mauritius, falling an easy prey to visiting seamen. In about 1638 a captive Dodo was to be seen in London, its apparent appetite for eating small pebbles exciting no small curiosity among the local citizens. It may have been this bird which ended up in the museum established by John Tradescant, gardener to Charles II, which was later incorporated into the collections of the Ashmolean Museum at Oxford. The head and right foot are all that survive of this historic specimen today and only a few fragmentary remains exist elsewhere. All other so-called Dodos exhibited in museums are fakes.

It is necessary to examine pictures painted long ago by painters who could have seen living Dodos to get some idea of the appearance of these ungainly birds. Unfortunately even these pictures are unreliable because most of them seem to have been painted from dead and stuffed specimens. This painting by George Edwards is not likely to be an accurate portrait of the Dodo (the beak, for instance, was less hooked than he represents it) but it is still one of the most charming and endurable of the many which have been attempted.

The Dodo.

Geo Edwards, Sculp: AD. 1757.

294

Tawny Owl

TAWNY OWL, *Strix aluco*. Hand coloured engraving probably by Violante Vanni pl. 94 from Vol. 1 of Xaverio Manetti's *Ornithologia Methodice Digesta*, 1767–76. Size of plate 13½″ × 10½″.

It is tempting to regard this curious picture as an ornithological joke, a little bit of nonsense. No owl ever looked like this, except in the artist's mind. It is almost as though we are contemplating an owl dressed in a caricature of a convict's outfit. But can we be sure that the artist was merely being playful? Surely not. Manetti's book would have been time-consuming and costly to produce and there are many cheaper and simpler ways to have fun. So there may have been a serious purpose behind this seemingly light-hearted publication.

At the same time as Manetti was publishing his five large volumes on birds at Florence a woman was working on a bird book at Rome. Published in 1775 in one volume Maddalena Bouchard's treatise seems to have been inspired entirely by Manetti's. Included in it is a picture of the Tawny Owl identical to Manetti's except for additional embellishments in the shape of a plant and a couple of unconvincing insects. Edward Lear, lover of owls and nonsense, would have approved of Mannetti's Tawny Owl and Maddalena Bouchard's blatant copy of it.

Strige maggiore, o Strige Allocco. ——— *Strix maior, sive Strix Aluco.*

All'Illmo Sig.^{re} M^{se}, e Cav.^{re} Alessandro Coppoli Patrizio Fior.^{no} e Perugino.

Magnificent Frigate Bird

MAGNIFICENT FRIGATE BIRD, 'La Grande Fregate de Cayenne', *Fregata magnificens*. Hand coloured engraving by François-Nicolas Martinet, pl. 961 from Vol. 9 of G.L.L. de Buffon's *Histoire Naturelle des Oiseaux* (with *Planches Enluminées* engraved by Martinet under the supervision of E.L. Daubenton), 1770–86. Size of plate 10″ × 8½″.

There are two good reasons for including this picture in this series of bird plates: it comes from an early and influential book illustrating hundreds of birds in colour; and it is a reasonably successful and, for its time, rare attempt by a land-based artist, working from his imagination and the accounts of sailors and travellers, to show a bird in flight.

The specific identity of the bird illustrated is not certain, but it is probably intended to be a female Magnificent Frigate Bird, the female of that species having her neck and throat picked out in white (the male, but for a bright red pouch over the throat, is all black); none of the other four Frigate Bird species seems to match up with the illustration.

With a seven-foot wingspan supporting a very light body, these buccaneers of the seas remain airborne for hours on end. They harass other sea birds in the air to rob them of their food and will even snatch chicks from other birds' nests, but they can also pluck flying fish and other creatures from the surface of the sea or just above it without landing on its surface or getting wet. They do not willingly enter the sea because their feathers become waterlogged very easily, making take-off difficult. As they usually stay fairly close to the shore, seamen have long regarded them favourably as reliable indicators of land.

961.

La grande Frégate, de Cayenne.

Yellowhammer

YELLOWHAMMER, *Emberiza citrinella*. Hand coloured engraving by Jan Christiaan Sepp, pl. 61 from Vol. 2 of C. Nozeman's *Nederlandsche Vogelen*, 1770–1829. Size of plate 16½″ × 10½″.

When Cornelis Nozeman embarked upon his grand scheme to illustrate and describe all the birds of the Netherlands he was fortunate to secure the services of a fine artist and engraver, Jan Christiaan Sepp, who is better known as an illustrator of fine books on insects. Then, as now, it often required a very good artist to make a lot out of a little to give certain natural history illustrations some impact. The Yellowhammer is a small bird and Nozeman's book was folio-sized. Here Sepp showed how it was possible to make an attractive compositon from two Yellowhammers, their nests and eggs, and a little ancillary foliage. Together with the carefully applied colouring, Sepp's designs ensured that Nozeman's book would for some years be well ahead of its time. They also made it an expensive production. When it was completed, 60 years after it had been started, it was on sale for 525 Dutch florins, making it the costliest book in the Netherlands in 1829.

Yellowhammers, in their breeding plumage anyway, are possibly the yellowest birds in Europe: at least, that is how it seems when you come across a flock of them feeding on the ground in the breeding season. The yellowness, it should be emphasized, is largely an attribute of the mature male birds, the females and the juveniles being noticeably less yellow. Two to six eggs are laid in a cup-shaped nest built by the female. Situated in a well-concealed place on the ground or in a bush a few feet above it, the nest is made of moss, grass and plant stems and is lined with grass and hair. It is unlikely that a Yellowhammer would or could construct such a neat, symmetrical and totally unprotected nest as the one shown in this picture.

Shelduck

SHELDUCK, *Anas tadorna* (now *Tadorna tadorna*). Hand coloured engraving by Jan Christiaan Sepp, pl. 100 from Vol. 2 of C. Nozeman's *Nederlandsche Vogelen*, 1770–1829. Size of plate 16½″ × 10½″.

In the second half of the eighteenth century Cornelis Nozeman, a Dutch clergyman, set out to illustrate and describe all the birds known in the Netherlands. Conceived on a grand scale, his book was embellished with hand coloured engravings illustrating males and females of the various species, often with figures of their nests and eggs. But, as has often happened with ambitious natural history publications, Nozeman had bitten off more than he could chew: he died in 1786 leaving the job only half completed (Martin Houttuyn finished it in 1829).

This plate, published three years after Nozeman's death, shows just one bird, a female Shelduck, and – a typical Sepp touch – a single egg, shown as an inset drawing pinned to a wall (a clutch usually contains from 8–15 eggs). As with most of the plates to this elegant and rare work the colouring has been applied meticulously and is close to nature. Even the goose-like appearance of Nozeman's Shelduck is acceptable because this bird can resemble a goose, especially when flying.

The Shelduck is a common bird of estuaries and coastal flats over much of western and southern Europe and as a migrant is even seen as far afield as India and the Far East. The mature male bird, or drake, is similar in most respects to the female but has a large red knob on its bill.

ANAS TADORNA, Foemina.

Guianan Cock-of-the-Rock

GUIANAN COCK-OF-THE-ROCK, *Rupicola rupicola*. Colour printed engraving by Gremillet, finished with watercolours, after a drawing by Jacques Barraband, pl. 51 from Vol. 1 of François Levaillant's *Histoire Naturelle des Oiseaux de Paradis &c.*, 1801–06. Size of plate 20½″ × 14″.

François Levaillant, a prolific author of bird books, was very well served by Jacques Barraband, many of whose wonderful watercolours are represented by engravings in his books. Among the most accomplished of Barraband's drawings were those included in Levaillant's book about Birds of Paradise in which they were very well engraved by Gremillet. The plate reproduced here comes from that book, although the bird depicted is not a Bird of Paradise from New Guinea but belongs to a South American family known as the Chatterers, and comes from the Guianas and Brazil.

Measuring about twelve inches long, the male Guianan Cock-of-the-Rock is a truly magnificent creature, its plumage being a bright orange-red colour (the female is uniformly brown). Both sexes have a crest which may be erected at will.

Males congregate when the courtship season arrives and perform a spectacular dance, having previously cleared the ground of debris. Early in the day an old male bird drops from a branch on to the ground and starts leaping about, then stands still with his tail fanned out and his wings spread, and then starts leaping about again, and so on all day. About seven or eight other males follow suit and they keep up this acrobatic, puzzling perform-ance well into the morning. It is a courtship dance of some kind but its precise purpose is still not clearly understood, especially since it is often performed after the eggs have been laid and have hatched.

Le Coq de roche mâle. N.º 51.

Barraband pinx.t   De l'Imprimerie de Rousset.   Grémilier sculp.t

Yellow-crowned Night Heron and others

YELLOW-CROWNED HERON, *Nycticorax violaceus* (now Yellow-crowned Night Heron); Great Heron, *Ardea herodias* (now Great Blue Heron); American Bittern, *Botaurus lentiginosus*; Least Bittern, *Ixobrychus exilis*. Hand coloured engraving by A.G. Warnicke, pl. 65 from Vol. 8 of Alexander Wilson's *American Ornithology*, 1808–14. Size of plate 13¼″ × 10¼″.

A wonderful display of artistic accomplishment is not to be found in this plate; it is rather to be seen as the result of an honest endeavour which helped make ornithological history. If Alexander Wilson had not entered John James Audubon's frontier store in 1810 it is possible that the latter would never have been stimulated to publish his *Birds of America*. In that event Wilson's own *American Ornithology* would probably be more celebrated now than it is. But it was destined always to be overshadowed – some would say eclipsed – by Audubon's admittedly much more impressive book. Nevertheless, Wilson's *American Ornithology* has great merit as a pioneering treatise on American birds and has the distinction of being the first full-length study of the subject to be produced entirely on American territory.

This plate is a typical example of Wilson's handiwork, the birds being displayed to facilitate identification rather than to create an artistic impression. It lacks the bravura of an Audubon plate but has a quiet charm which may reflect the personality of Alexander Wilson himself, the acknowledged father of American ornithology. The greatness of this plate lies in its honesty.

Drawn from Nature by A. Wilson. 1. Yellow-crowned Heron.   2. Great Heron.   3. American Bittern.   4. Least B.   Engraved by I. G. Warnicke.

65

Common Coot

COMMON COOT, *Fulica atra*. Hand coloured engraving by W.H. Lizars, pl. 32 from Vol. 2 of P.J. Selby's *Illustrations of British Ornithology*, 1819–34. Size of plate 21" × 16½".

With its sombre plumage, relieved only by its white forehead and white bill, the Common Coot is not one of the outstanding beauties of the bird world, especially when it is shown out of water. Presumably Selby wanted to display all the bird's external features or needed to show it at full stretch to help fill up the extra large plate, for it measures only about fifteen inches from the end of its dumpy bill to the end of its stubby tail. But at least this rather inelegant view of it shows off its curious feet to advantage. As in all Coots the toes are edged with fleshy lobes or membranes which increase its swimming and paddling abilities.

The Common Coots of Britain and France do not travel far as a rule, but those from more northern districts of Europe migrate south in cold weather to northern Africa and the Middle East, some travelling as far as South-east Asia. Although they do not look capable of sustained flight they can cover distances of 250 miles or more overnight. The migrant birds sometimes congregate in large numbers at suitable places and are often seen in the company of ducks. Most of the time, however, the Common Coot may be seen at large pools, creeks and still streams, where it swims or jump-dives for its food, which comprises fish, various invertebrates and aquatic plants. The bulky nest, constructed by both parents, is usually placed among reeds and aquatic vegetation and may be free-floating. For all its adventurous qualities it is still a very domestic-looking creature.

PLATE XXXVII.

White-fronted Goose

WHITE-FRONTED GOOSE, *Anser albifrons*. Hand coloured engraving by W. H. Lizars, pl. 43 from Vol. 2 of P.J. Selby's *Illustrations of British Ornithology*, 1821–34. Size of plate 21″ × 16½″.

Prideaux John Selby was the Audubon of Great Britain, each plate of his *Illustrations of British Ornithology* occupying only a few square inches less space than each plate of *The Birds of America*. Like Audubon he intended showing each bird of the natural size: unlike Audubon he was unable to do so consistently. Like Audubon, too, he chose the gifted William Home Lizars to engrave his plates: unlike Audubon he allowed Lizars to finish the job.

The White-fronted Goose, a bird which may attain a length of 30 inches, could not be accommodated on Selby's plate natural size but it does fill it impressively. The orange-yellow bill and dark-coloured plumage are typical of the Greenland race of the bird, which tends to winter in Ireland and western Scotland; but the broad white forehead occurs on all White-fronted Geese and is diagnostic. One of five similar species known as 'grey geese' it has its breeding grounds in the subarctic tundra, which helps explain why human beings have not been able to exterminate it.

Many years after this engraving was published artists such as the late Sir Peter Scott gave us pictures showing how impressive this goose and others like it appear in flight. Selby merely followed the conventions of his time by showing his White-fronted Goose waddling uncomfortably on land.

PLATE XLIII.

WHITE FRONTED WILD GOOSE.

Ocellated Turkey

OCELLATED TURKEY, *Agriocharis ocellata*. Hand coloured engraving by Nicholas Huet, pl. 112 from C.J. Temminck and M. Laugier de Chartrouse's *Nouveau Recueil de Planches Coloriées d'Oiseaux*, 1820–39. Size of plate 10½″ × 8¼″.

Although considerably smaller than the Domesticated Turkey this is still a fairly large bird, measuring 36 to 40 inches in length, the cock bird being larger than the hen. It gets its name from the blue 'eyes', outlined with black, decorating the tail feathers. It was described at the beginning of the nineteenth century: this picture of it, by Nicholas Huet, was probably the first to be published and remains one of the best; copies of it were still appearing in natural history books many years later.

Always considered a scarce bird, the Ocellated Turkey lives in thick forest in parts of Central America and Mexico (where the Domesticated Turkey is also believed to have originated). It has long been persecuted by hunters and, together with the destruction of much of its living space, this could soon lead to its extinction in the wild state. Fortunately it has been reared successfully in captivity in recent years. Considering its size and conspicuous coloration it is amazing that the Ocellated Turkey has until now survived the ferocity of its human persecutors in its native haunts and comforting to know that it is likely to live on happily in zoos and bird gardens elsewhere.

112.

Dindon *œuillé*.

Huet.

Ostrich

BLACK OSTRICH (now Ostrich, *Struthio camelus*). Hand coloured engraving, pl. 139 from Vol. 8 of John Latham's *A General History of Birds*, 1821–24. Size of plate 7″ × 5″.

Standing eight feet tall and weighing up to 345 pounds, the Ostrich is the largest bird in the world. Although several different races have been described they all belong to the same species, the only surviving member of a family which once ranged from southern Europe to Mongolia. It has managed to survive in Africa, a continent full of formidable predators, partly because it can fight but mostly because it has a remarkable turn of speed, about 30 miles an hour at maximum. Generally it roams the African plains in small groups and is often seen in the company of gnus, zebras and other harmless mammals. It is almost omnivorous and is attracted by glass and shiny, metallic objects which it swallows with apparent impunity.

For centuries it has been slaughtered for its feathers, even though these may be removed from the bird without harming it, the sixteen plumes on each wing being purely decorative and replaceable. The Ostrich may also be trained for riding and to pull carriages and carts, though it has little staying power. As may be expected of the world's largest bird its egg is also the largest of any existing bird – even though it is smaller in relation to body size than any other bird's egg.

According to the English ornithologist John Latham, who published this rather formal picture of what he called the Black Ostrich, 'None but the Africans will eat the flesh, but these esteem it a delicacy, and the fat is used in cookery; the eggs also are eaten, and the shells suspended under the vaulted roofs, not only of the Mahometan mosques, but also of the Greek and Coptic churches; and would indeed be esteemed a beautiful ornament everywhere, was the difficulty of procuring them greater.' Unfortunately the fine, soft skin of this giant among birds also appeals to its human predators; these find it admirably suited to the manufacture of fancy items such as gloves and purses. The largest bird in the world, it seems, lives only to be persecuted.

Black Ostrich.

Andean Condor

ANDEAN CONDOR, *Cathartes gryphus* (now *Vultur gryphus*). Hand coloured engraving, pl. 1 from Vol. 4 of Charles Lucien Bonaparte's *American Ornithology; or the Natural History of the Birds Inhabiting the United States not given by Wilson*, 1825–33. Size of plate 13½″ × 10½″.

With a wingspan of almost ten feet the Andean Condor is one of the largest of flying birds, only the wingspan of the Wandering Albatross being a few inches greater. One of half-a-dozen different Condors, its ability to soar for long periods at great heights is equalled only by the great Californian Condor. It lives in the high Andes and ranges from Venezuela to the Magellan Straits.

The nest is made on almost inaccessible ledges on rocky cliffs in the mountains and two eggs are laid in it. The birds remain in the nest for a long time and do not breed until they are six years old, but they may live for at least fifty years. They have a highly developed sense of smell but seem to be able to locate food at distances of up to a mile by sight and will congregate over the carcass of a dying animal.

In his text accompanying this engraving of a young male, the eminent Corsican naturalist Charles Lucien Bonaparte drew attention to the extraordinary persistence of a legend concerning this impressive bird: 'it is almost incredible,' he said, 'and remarkably illustrates the force of preconceived opinions, that in the year 1830, a traveller could be found with assurance enough to impose upon us, and journals, even of respectable standing, to copy as positive and authentic, a description of a Condor of *moderate size*, just killed, and actually lying before the narrator, so large that a single quill-feather was twenty good paces long! This might indeed have lifted an Elephant . . . ' Perhaps the sight of a bird with a ten-foot wingspan has a powerful effect on the imagination.

Drawn from Nature by A. Rider.

Young Male Condor.
Cathartes Gryphus.
22

Engraved by Alexander Lawson.

Indian Courser

Coromandel Courier, *Cursorius asiaticus* (now Indian Courser, *Cursorius coromandelicus*). Hand coloured engraving by W.H. Lizars, pl. 22 from James Wilson's *Illustrations of Zoology*, 1827. Size of plate 16¼″ × 12¼″.

James Wilson wrote mostly about obscure aspects of natural history, his most substantial contribution to knowledge being his *Illustrations of Zoology*, a miscellaneous collection of pictures of little-known animals, with commentary. The Scotsman thought it was worth publishing an engraving of one of the nine species of Coursers, this one living in dry, sandy places in northern Sri Lanka and India. An earlier name for the eastern coast of Madras was Coromandel, which accounts for the scientific name of the bird.

Coursers all have long legs and are found in arid or semi-arid regions where they run about rapidly looking for insects. Occasionally they will stop and stretch their necks upwards to obtain a larger view of the horizon. Conversely, when they feel threatened, they crouch down and rely on their excellent camouflage to protect them. This picture apparently represents a bird in its surveying posture but the artist may have drawn from a specimen which had been stuffed by a taxidermist who had never seen a living Indian Courser.

PLATE XXII.

Drawn by James Wilson.

The Cream-coloured Plover. CURSORIUS ASIATICUS.

Eng.d by W. H. Lizars.

Brown Thrasher

FERRUGINOUS THRUSH, *Turdus rufus* (now Brown Thrasher, *Toxostoma rufum*). Hand coloured aquatint by John James Audubon and Robert Havell, pl. 116 from Vol. 2 of Audubon's *The Birds of America*, 1827–38. Size of plate 38¼″ × 25⅝″.

Theatricality is the unique feature distinguishing John James Audubon's art from that of most other bird artists. Often his birds seem to be acting out parts in dramas and comedies set among woods, fields, marshes, seashores and deserts. Heroes, villains, wise men, thieves, singers and scolders seem to strut and flap through every other page of his great book. Nowhere does this sense of theatre shine through more eloquently than in this plate.

An uncritical glance shows us a Black Snake entwined around the branch of an oak tree (which also supports a nest with eggs) being attacked by three Brown Thrashers, a fourth lying apparently lifeless over a coil of the snake. Can this be an everyday scene in the life of the Brown Thrasher? It seems most unlikely. On the other hand it may remind us of a dramatic scene recalled from visits to art galleries or from pictures in books illustrating epic stories from classical writers. The female bird lying limply over the snake's body is a damsel in distress, the female above is being threatened by the snake – the villainous dragon of the piece – and the two males are behaving heroically.

The picture could be an ornithological version of the Perseus and Andromeda myth, except that there are two heroes and two heroines. Audubon's brief sojourn in the Paris atelier of the painter Jacques Louis David may have given him a taste for such dramatic scenes, but he may also have had an intuitive grasp of theatre. Either way he is unlikely to have been a witness of scenes such as that depicted here.

Ferruginous Thrush.

TURDUS RUFUS. *Linn.*

Male, 1. Female, 2.

Black jack Oak. Quercus nigra.

Black Snake.

Trumpeter Swan

TRUMPETER SWAN, *Cygnus buccinator* (now Olor *buccinator*). Hand coloured aquatint by John James Audubon and Robert Havell, pl. 406 from Vol. 4 of Audubon's *The Birds of America*, 1827–38. Size of plate 38¼" × 25⅝".

The Trumpeter Swan is one of the most magnificent birds of North America and Audubon portrayed it memorably in this plate. In his day it would have been a familiar sight, so it is surprising that he did not paint this picture of it for his book until 1836 or 1837, towards the end of his self-appointed task to illustrate all the birds of his adopted country. The Trumpeter Swan once ranged as far south as Missouri but, because it has been hunted ruthlessly for sport, is now almost entirely restricted to parts of Canada and sanctuaries in several national parks in western parts of the United States (although it winters as far south as southern California and Texas). The mature bird is about six feet in length and has a wing span of up to ten feet, so it is an easy target.

As with some of his other illustrations of the larger birds, each of which he wanted to show of the natural size, Audubon painted his subject with its head turned upon itself and artfully introduced a tasty moth to justify such a pose. That the pose is also aesthetically satisfying is indicated by the prices which have been obtained at auction for this plate alone. In 1983 a copy of it made $45,000 and in 1987 another made $48,000, prices which have been exceeded by only two or three other prints of natural history subjects – each of them from *The Birds of America*. If the propaganda value of Audubon's memorable picture has helped save the Trumpeter Swan from extinction, as it probably has, then truly the brush may be mightier than the sportsman's rifle – a comforting thought.

Trumpeter Swan.
CYGNUS BUCCINATOR
Adult.

Greater Flamingo

AMERICAN FLAMINGO, *Phoenicopterus ruber* (now Greater Flamingo). Hand coloured aquatint by John James Audubon and Robert Havell, pl. 431 from Vol. 4 of Audubon's *The Birds of America*, 1827–38. Size of plate 38¼″ × 25⅝″.

The most famous bird book in the world is *The Birds of America* by John James Audubon. One of the best known pictures in it is that of the Greater Flamingo. In the United States at least this picture is better known than Dürer's *Rhinoceros* or Landseer's *Monarch of the Glen*. Because Audubon wanted to show his birds at their natural size he was often compelled to display them in apparently unnatural, cramped attitudes, despite the enormous size of his plates; so his Greater Flamingo looks as though bent unnaturally double, its long neck mirroring its left leg. There is a quirkiness about it, difficult to define, which is evident in many of Audubon's bird portraits. It seems to have strayed on to the plate from a Walt Disney cartoon. It could almost be an ornithological joke, but it is not.

Because of the imposed page size of his monumental treatise, the largest size practicable for a printed book, Audubon could not have portrayed his Flamingo at natural size with its head held high, assuming he had wanted to; and he did not want to reduce the bird to fit the page. What seems a quirky compromise is close to the attitude often adopted by the bird in real life. Stephen Jay Gould, a distinguished American biologist, has pointed out that Audubon's haughty Flamingo, when turned upside down and deprived of its legs, becomes a happy swan, a transformation made possibly only because Audubon drew his Flamingo accurately; and he drew it accurately because he had observed it well.

Audubon took immense pains over his bird pictures, from the original field sketches to the minutiae of the printed plates. The results are occasionally unnatural in some respects but his Flamingo is entirely satisfactory and has become one of the most enduring of his many bird portraits.

PLATE CCCXXXI.

1... Profile view of Bill at its greatest extension.
2... Superior front view of upper Mandible.
3... Inferior front view of upper Mandible.
4... Inferior front view of lower Mandible.
5... Inferior front view of lower Mandible with the Tongue in.

6... Profile view of Tongue.
7... Superior front view of Tongue.
8... Inferior front view of Tongue.
9... Perpendicular front view of the feet fully expanded.

American Flamingo.
PHŒNICOPTERUS RUBER, *Linn.*
Old Male.

Red Bishop

RED BISHOP, *Fringilla ignicolor* (now *Euplectes orix franciscanus*). Hand coloured engraving, pl.2 (from the *Aves* volume, 1828) of Christian Gottfried Ehrenberg's *Symbolae Physicae*, 1828–45. Size of plate 19¼″ × 12¾″.

The Red Bishop (also known as the Red-throated Bishop-bird or Orange Bishop) is one of the most brilliantly coloured of the Weaver-birds, so called from the often complex nests which many of them weave high up in trees. By far the greater number of Weaver-birds (which are closely related to the ubiquitous House Sparrow) come from Africa, where some of them have become serious pests because they consume useful seeds in great quantity. Even the widespread use of flame throwers and chemicals sprayed from aircraft has not markedly diminished their numbers. The five-inch-long Red Bishop is also very fond of termites and destroys vast numbers of them, but it is still regarded as a nuisance, albeit a pretty one.

It is the male Red Bishop, as would be expected, which sports the bright colouring, though after moulting the red plumage gradually disappears and has been known to become almost black; the seed diet may be responsible for the colour change. The females are rather colourless but the male is happy to gather about him a harem of two or three – he seems to have done so in this illustration – and he bounces about in front of them while making clapping noises with his wings. The nest is constructed among reed beds or in wet marshes and resembles an elongated cup without a handle suspended between reeds; the hole in the side for access is shown in this picture. The artist's vignette to the side of the nest shows a clutch of four blue eggs but normally there are two or three eggs in a clutch. Red Bishops are found from Senegal to Ethiopia and throughout eastern Africa.

FRINGILLA *ignicolor.*

Dongata.

Müller pinxit.

Schmidt in lapidem deliniavit.

Major Mitchell's Cockatoo

LEADBEATER'S COCKATOO, *Plyctolophus leadbeateri* (now Major Mitchell's Cockatoo, *Cacatua leadbeateri*). Hand coloured lithograph by Edward Lear, pl. 5 from his *Illustrations of the Family of Psittacidae, or Parrots*, 1830–32. Size of plate 19½″ × 13″.

It is not surprising that Edward Lear should have included this bird in his monograph for it is possibly the most beautiful of all the Cockatoos. His illustration of it is a minor masterpiece which must have given him much satisfaction. The delicate pink suffusing the bird's plumage must have been especially difficult for the colourists to duplicate successfully on each of the 175 copies of the plate which were produced. But it is the less delicately coloured crest which makes Major Mitchell's Cockatoo a favourite with aviculturists, who must part with a lot of money for the privilege of owning one.

This bird was originally named after Mr Leadbeater, a dealer in bird skins who lent parrots to Lear in addition to those on view at the London Zoo. It is found in the wild in western and central parts of Australia and may be locally common but is becoming scarcer throughout its range. Fortunately it is a sturdy and adaptable species in captivity.

While he drew birds in the parrot house of the London Zoo Lear used to satisfy the curiosity of members of the public by making rapid cartoon sketches of their faces and this practice may have been the genesis of the comic characters which embellish his books of nonsense verse, books which brought him more fame in his lifetime than did his illustrations of birds. Nowadays, however, we are more impressed by his picture of Major Mitchell's Cockatoo than by his Dong with the Luminous Nose.

PLYCTOLOPHUS LEADBEATERI.

Leadbeater's Cockatoo.

E. Lear del et lith.   Printed by C. Hullmandel.

Scarlet Macaw

RED AND YELLOW MACAW, *Macrocercus aracanga* (now Scarlet Macaw, *Ara macao*). Hand coloured lithograph by Edward Lear, pl. 7 from his *Illustrations of the Family of Psittacidae, or Parrots*, 1830–32. Size of plate 19½" × 13".

As a boy Edward Lear filled notebooks with sketches of natural objects such as flowers, feathers, fish, shells and birds. The future author of *A Book of Nonsense* was born with an intense love of nature. By the time he was fifteen he was selling sketches and colouring prints and fans to earn a few shillings a week. Shortly afterwards, about 1829, he was experimenting with lithography and had begun planning a book about parrots, intending to illustrate all the species then known.

Working mostly from living parrots in the Zoological Gardens at London's Regent's Park he published a total of 43 plates between 1830 and 1832 and then abandoned the project; his eyesight, never very good, was not up to the exacting task of showing the fine details he worked into every drawing. Among the 42 bird portraits, however, were several which have never been equalled for beauty and accuracy. As only 175 copies of the book were marketed it is now very rare and desirable. This partly explains why it now sells for staggeringly high prices ($190,000 was paid for a copy at auction in June 1989). The fame of its author as a writer of nonsense has also helped push up the price of this, his first and rarest book.

This is probably the most outstanding and the most popular of Lear's parrot studies. Several preliminary sketches for it exist, which show how meticulous he was over details of plumage and colour. The job of colouring the final lithographs was undertaken by assistants working under his supervision.

The Scarlet Macaw, probably the best known of the fifteen macaw species, is found from Bolivia to Mexico and is a familiar sight in zoos and bird gardens. When mature it measures about 36 inches from its beak to the tip of its tail. Its slightly disdainful expression may be attributed to the lack of feathers on its face, which is covered with a whitish skin.

MACROCERCUS ARACANGA.

Red and Yellow Maccaw.

¾ Nat. Size.

Western Tragopan

BLACK-HEADED HORNED PHEASANT, *Satyra melanocephala* (now Western Tragopan, *Tragopan melanocephalus*). Hand coloured lithograph by William Hawkins, pl. 48 from Vol. 1 of J.E. Gray's *Illustrations of Indian Zoology*, 1830–35. Size of plate 18″ × 12½″.

This is probably the first published illustration of the bird now known as the Western Tragopan. It is not an entirely accurate representation of the bird, the fleshy 'horns' in particular being exaggerated (they are less rigid and less raised than they look here). The lithographer, William Hawkins, may have had to copy a drawing which had been done by a native Indian artist whose artistic training and outlook would have differed radically from his; and as the bird was almost certainly unknown in the West in the 1830s errors in the drawing would have been perpetuated unintentionally.

The first live specimens of the Western Tragopan were brought to Europe in 1864 and for a time the bird bred successfully; it is doubtful that any are living in captivity in Europe now. As its natural habitat is in a restricted part of the north-western Himalayas it will be difficult to obtain further examples to establish a breeding stock. Tragopans, as this illustration suggests, are pheasants and, like most pheasants, they often sit on branches; unlike other pheasants they build bulky nests of twigs in thick bushes and low trees.

Drawn & lith. by W. Hawkins.

Printed by Engelmann & Co.

BLACK HEADED HORNED PHEASANT. SATYRA MELANOCEPHALA.
Adult male.

Short-eared Owl and Great Horned Owl

SHORT-EARED OWL, *Strix brachyota* (top, now *Asio flammeus*); Arctic White-horned Owl, *Strix arctica* (bottom, now Great Horned Owl, *Bubo virginianus arcticus*). Hand coloured engraving by S. Milne after a drawing by Thomas Brown, pl. 18 from Brown's *Illustrations of the American Ornithology of Alexander Wilson and Lucian Bonaparte*, 1831–35. Size of plate 16″ × 12½″.

Looked upon merely as decoration this plate has a pleasing quality. As an original contribution to natural history, however, it may be criticised. The description of our Plate 55, also reproduced from *Illustrations of the American Ornithology*, shows that Thomas Brown tended to adapt illustrations from the publications of others to suit his own ends. Further evidence of that tendency is provided by this plate. The figure of the Short-eared Owl staring out at us has been pillaged from one of Brown's favourite store-houses of bird portraits, Audubon's *Birds of America*, and has lost some of the artistic bravura of the original in the process.

Brown's figure of the so-called Arctic Owl perched upon a magnolia is not entirely convincing, but research has shown that this, too, has been appropriated from another publication, without acknowledgment. The source of this figure is a volume on the birds of North America, published in London in 1831, part of the *Fauna Boreali Americana* edited by Sir John Richardson. William Swainson, a talented artist, illustrated the volume and one of the illustrations is a figure of the Arctic Owl (a form of the Great Horned Owl), almost identical in its main features to Brown's figure. This was such a rare bird in Brown's day – even more so in ours – that he had little option but to copy Swainson's published figure of it. But why did Brown show this bird of cold northern latitudes perched upon a magnolia, a plant from the warm south? The reason for this curious juxtaposition of opposites may not be far to seek. The sub-title of his book suggests that, besides figures of birds, it was supposed to include figures of all the forest trees of North America. He needed to place a magnolia somewhere and he needed a perch for his Arctic Owl, so he brought the two together in a marriage of convenience. Brown's book may not be very reliable but it is very entertaining – and very pleasing on the eye.

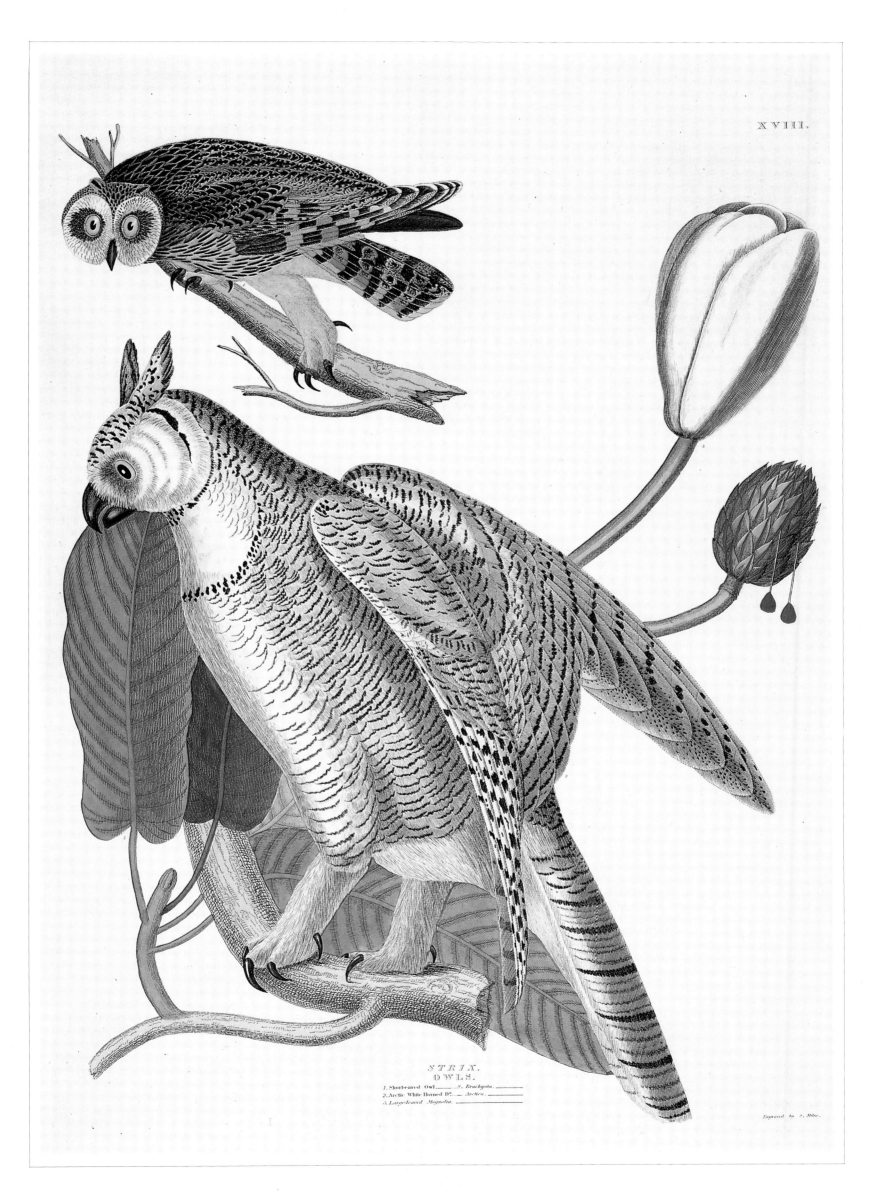

STRIX.
OWLS.

1. Short-eared Owl. ___ *S. Brachyota.* _____
2. Arctic White Horned D?. ___ *Arctica.* _____
3. Large-leaved *Magnolia.* _____

Engraved by S. Milne.

Short-billed Jay and others

SHORT-BILLED JAY (top left, identification uncertain); Columbian Jay (top right, now Collie's Magpie-Jay, *Callocita colliei*; American Magpie (bottom left, now Magpie, *Pica pica*). Hand coloured engraving by S. Milne after a drawing by Thomas Brown, pl. 20 from Brown's *Illustrations of the American Ornithology of Alexander Wilson and Charles Lucian Bonaparte*, 1831–35. Size of plate 16″ × 12½″.

Most of the natural history publications of Captain Thomas Brown were based unashamedly on the works of others. Hack writer, illustrator and experienced, if uncritical, naturalist, Brown calmly appropriated illustrations of animals and plants which had appeared elsewhere and adapted them for his own pot-boilers. The figure of the Mexican bird on the right of this plate, for instance, was almost certainly adapted from Audubon's *Birds of America*, in which book it had just been published in the mistaken belief that it had come from the Columbia River region hundreds of miles to the north; Audubon had used a stuffed specimen, obtained for him by a friend, as a model. Brown, sublimely unaware that he was perpetuating Audubon's error, was only interested in making a colourful and well composed plate.

With all its faults Brown's book is a most attractive production, this plate being only one of many which are easy on the eye. It has always been a very rare book and is a high spot in any ornithological library.

XX.

GARRULUS.
JAYS.
1. Short-billed Jay.   G. Brachyrynchus.
2. Columbian   D?.   — Bullockii.
3. Magpie.   — Pica.
,. White-flowered Stuartia.

J. Mavson Sc.

Eagle Owl

EAGLE OWL, *Bubo bubo*. Hand coloured lithograph by Edward Lear, pl. 37 from Vol. 1 of John Gould's *The Birds of Europe*, 1832–37. Size of plate 21½″ × 14″.

Magnificent though it is, this picture of an Eagle Owl by Edward Lear makes the bird look unreal, almost a caricature of what it should look like, for no nocturnal bird of prey is stronger or more formidable.

In a poetic passage, John Gould outlines a scenario for this noble bird's predatory behaviour: 'Perched upon some branch, and observed by the shadows of the evening, it marks its ill-fated quarry – the fawn reposing among the fern – the hare nibbling the grass – the grouse couching among the heath; silently and rapidly down it pounces, strikes its talons into its victim, and commences the work of destruction. Less noble game, such as moles, rats and lizards, may be also ranked among its articles of food.'

This is still a common bird in parts of its range, which comprises Scandinavia, much of Russia, Europe south to the Pyrenees, Italy and Greece, but it is not often visible to the casual onlooker. In the daylight hours it is inclined to rest motionless in an upright position close to the trunk of a conifer, where its protective coloration makes its outline difficult to see. For all its ferocity the Eagle Owl can become very tame and has been known to live in captivity for 60 years or more. On the other hand, it may revert to its naturally savage state if its nest or its progeny are approached too closely.

Although Lear did not capture the latent ferocity of this bird his picture of it may well be the most memorable ever painted. But did his subject really look at him like that? The bespectacled, mild-mannered and inquisitive Lear regarded himself as owl-like, so it is just possible that this was an unintentional self portrait; Lear's Eagle Owl could be Lear himself!

EAGLE OWL.
Bubo maximus (Sibbald)

Drawn from Nature by E. Lear.   Printed by C. Hullmandel.

Celebes Hornbill and others

CARBUNCLED HORNBILL, *Buceros cassidix* (now Celebes Hornbill, *Aceros cassidix* and other Hornbills. Hand coloured engraving by William Warwick after a drawing by Thomas Brown, pl. 99B from *The Edinburgh Journal of Natural History*, 1839. Size of plate 19″ × 12″.

In this plate we see several Hornbills, the central one being the Celebes Hornbill of what is now known as Sulawesi in Indonesia. The artist, Thomas Brown, has not only combined in one view representations of different species which would never be seen together (a common practice among natural history artists in all ages) but has 'borrowed' them all from earlier publications. Nevertheless, the composition has a decorative quality, the background details (added by the engraver) are original, and the plate gives us a glimpse of the work of a minor artist about whom very little is known.

These are not pretty birds but they are fascinating, not least because of the huge bill with its saw-tooth edges and its horny 'casque' from which the name Hornbill is derived. In most species the seemingly heavy bill and 'casque' on the head are hollow or filled with honeycomb-like cells. The long tail is seldom colourful, unlike the bill which may be bright yellow or red. Hornbills are also endowed with well-developed eyelashes, a peculiarity shared by very few other birds.

But there is something else about Hornbills which has always made forest dwellers in the tropics treat these birds with respect and sometimes with reverence. They fascinated the famous author of *The Malay Archipelago*. 'The extraordinary habit of the male', said Alfred Russell Wallace in 1869, 'in plastering up the female with her egg and feeding her during the whole time of incubation, and till the young one is fledged, is common to several of the large hornbills, and is one of those strange facts in natural history which are "stranger than fiction".' To incubate her eggs the female allows herself to be virtually imprisoned in a hole in a tree by the male, the hole being almost sealed with mud, dirt and regurgitated matter, until it is time for her to come and help collect food for the nestlings, when she is released. This curious habit has impressed primitive peoples so much that Hornbills are usually left unmolested by them and may be represented in their rites as symbols of purity and fidelity.

BUCEROS, HORNBILLS.
1. B. corrugatus . . Grooved H.
2. Buccinator . . Trumpet —
3. Hydrocorax . . Bontian —
4. lunatus . . Double-beaked
5. Cassidix . . Carbuncled —
6. atratus . . Black-crested

Fig.r Milne sc.

Landsc. Turrey sc.

Victoria Crowned Pigeon

Victoria Crowned Pigeon, *Goura steursii* (now *Goura victoria victoria*). Hand coloured lithograph by David William Mitchell, after a drawing by Benjamin Waterhouse Hawkins, pl. 120 from Vol. 2 of George Robert Gray's *The Genera of Birds*, 1844–49. Size of plate 15″ × 10½″.

This handsome bird, the size of a small turkey, is one of the monarchs of the pigeon world. It is one of three species of the genus *Goura*, which differ from other pigeons by their greater size, their beautiful crest, and by having sixteen instead of twelve tail feathers. Inhabitants of New Guinea and some of its neighbouring islands, the Crowned Pigeons feed upon berries, seeds and grains, which they seek on the ground. When disturbed they take to the wing and have the unfortunate habit of settling on exposed limbs of trees where they make easy targets for hunters, so it is hardly surprising that they have become uncommon close to human dwellings. Like all pigeons their flesh makes good eating and this does not help their chances of survival. The nest is constructed in a tree and two eggs are laid in it.

The gorgeous crest, this bird's crowning glory, comprises a series of blue feathers which are spatulate at their ends and have white tips. Another striking feature is the pair of ruby-red eyes. Gentle and tame in captivity, they like to roost in trees at night. The illustration reproduced here was based on a living bird kept in Lord Stanley's aviary at Knowsley near Liverpool. A living example of the Victoria Crowned Pigeon must have been a rare sight in western Europe in the 1840s. It may soon be a rare sight anywhere.

GOURA
Steursii (Temm.)

Bullfinch

BULLFINCH, *Pyrrhula pyrrhula* Hand coloured engraving, pl. 11 from Vol. 1 of the second edition of James Bolton's *Harmonia Ruralis; or an Essay towards a Natural History of British Song Birds*, 1845. Size of plate 9" × 7".

James Bolton was an amateur naturalist from the north of England who wrote and illustrated several books about aspects of British natural history. His book on song birds was first published in the 1790s but was considered original enough to be reissued 50 years later. The illustrations are prettily evocative of their subjects, though they are unquestionably eighteenth century rather than nineteenth century in feeling. Those in the second edition of the book, published in 1845, would have contrasted strangely with the magnificent folio productions of John Gould, several of which were on sale by that date.

The Bullfinch rightly deserves a place in a book on song birds because, although it is only a moderately appealing songster in the wild, it learns to whistle simple tunes when in captivity. Its musical ability and its attractive coloration ensured that it would make a popular cage bird. On the other hand it is unpopular with owners of fruit trees because it feeds on buds.

Bullfinch or Nope.

Common Rhea

AMERICAN EMU, *Rhea americana* (now Common Rhea). Hand coloured lithograph by J.W. Moore after a drawing by Edward Lear, pl. 12 from Vol. 1 of J.E. Gray's *Gleanings from the Knowsley Menagerie and Aviary at Knowsley Hall*, 1846–50. Size of plate 21¾″ × 14½″.

The outstanding feature of this lithograph, based on a drawing by Edward Lear, is the way a five-foot tall bird is made to appear even taller than it is by the employment of a low viewpoint and the placing of it, correctly, in a seemingly limitless landscape. Lear's original watercolour reveals this sense of space even more dramatically than the published lithograph. The Rhea lives on the scrub and pampas plains of South America where it is very much at home, feeding largely on grass, insects and small vertebrates, and running, unhindered, at great speed over the wide open spaces.

In spite of their considerable turn of speed Rheas are not fast enough to elude capture by natives, who hunt them constantly. Many years ago they were hunted with the bolas, three heavy weights joined by long cords to a common centre. This contraption was hurled with great dexterity by a native on horseback, the cords winding about the bird's legs and bringing it down. Because Rheas are so tasty, particularly as young birds, their numbers are decreasing alarmingly and they require protection now if they are to survive in the wild. Their feathers, sad to tell, are put to an undignified use: they are bound up in bunches and used as brooms. At least Lear's magnificent study helps restore some dignity to this, one of the world's largest birds.

AMERICAN EMU.—RHEA AMERICANA.

Hullmandel & Walton Lithographers

Pileated Guan

PILEATED GUAN, *Penelope pileata* (also known as Green-backed Guan). Hand coloured lithograph by J.W.Moore after a drawing by Edward Lear, pl. 9 from Vol. 1 of J.E. Gray's *Gleanings from the Knowsley Menagerie and Aviary at Knowsley Hall*, 1846–50. Size of plate 21¾″ × 14½″.

Edward Lear spent five of the happiest years of his life working for Lord Stanley at Knowsley Hall, near Liverpool. Lord Stanley was very interested in acquiring new animals for his menagerie and aviary and tried, often successfully, to get them to adapt to the Engish climate. At Knowsley Lear completed many watercolours of birds, including the Pileated Guan. The example he drew seems to have been in good shape when it sat for its portrait and shows that this species, like other Guans, can successfully withstand the rigours of the European climate.

The Pileated Guan reaches a length of about 32 inches, large for a Guan though not large by comparison with some of its near relatives, the Curassows. One of fifteen known species of Guans, it is found in the Lower Amazon Valley of Brazil where it lives in small groups, a group sometimes comprising a single cock bird and a covey of hens. It is rather noisy, uttering unmusical cries similar to the braying of a donkey. In the early morning the cock bird will repeat his call for five minutes on end. No doubt Lear waited until it was in a quiet mood before sketching.

Plate 9.

Lear, del.

J. W. Moore, lithog.

PILEATED GUAN.—PENELOPE PILEATA.

Hullmandel & Walton Lithographers.

American Jacana

AMERICAN JACANA, *Parra cordifera* (now *Jacana spinosa*). Hand coloured lithograph by P. Oudart, pl. 42 from Marc A.P.O. Des Murs' *Iconographie Ornithologique*, 1849. Size of plate 14″ × 10″.

The eight species of Jacanas (pronounced zha–sa–nas) have several features which distinguish them from other birds, for example their spider-like, long-clawed toes. They are also known as 'lily-trotters' or 'lotus birds' because they walk on water-lily leaves and other vegetation; they do so habitually and with consummate ease. The artist has shown them, uncharacteristically, on dry land.

Approach a Jacana closely and it is likely to remain so still that, in spite of its brilliant colouring, it may be very difficult to see. A Jacana usually lays four shiny eggs, dark brown and streaked with black; these benefit from a kind of waterproofing, a useful quality because they are often submerged, the nest being a loosely floating mass of vegetation which is easily swamped.

Three geographical races of the American Jacana occur in the West Indies and in the territory stretching south from Mexico to Panama, each race having a black head and a bright yellow frontal shield above the bill similar to that of the Coots. Also distinctive are the wing spurs, one of which is just visible in the illustration. These spurs, present in only a few other bird groups, are efficient fighting weapons.

Parra cordifera. *(Lesson)*

JACANA CORDIFÈRE.

P. Oudart, pinx.¹ et lith.

O. des Murs, direx.ᵗ

Des Murs' Wiretail

DES MURS' WIRETAIL, *Sylviorthorhynchus maluroides* (now *Sylviorthorhynchus desmursii*). Hand coloured lithograph by P. Oudart, pl. 45 from Marc Des Murs' *Iconographie Ornithologique*, 1849. Size of plate 14″ × 10½″.

Large and resplendent birds seem to bring out the best in bird artists, but John Gould's monograph of the Humming-birds in five massive folio volumes, which is acknowledged as his masterpiece, showed what artists could do with the smallest birds in the world. For small birds, too, may be resplendent or may have peculiarities which open up artistic possibilities. Des Murs' Wiretail, the size of a Wren, is one example.

An inhabitant of Chile and Argentina, it is one of more than 200 South American members of a family which includes birds, sometimes known as Woodhewers, with extravagantly long tails. It frequents woods and forests, is agile and light in its movements and can cling to the most slender and supple branches. Like many of its relatives it constructs a tunnel-like nest. Its extraordinary tail, which seems to have a purely ornamental function, remains vertical whether the bird is walking or jumping. Although closely related to many other birds sporting extravagant tail feathers, it is the only one with a tail resembling that of the Australian Lyrebirds. The feathers comprising the tail are so narrow they look more like wires, to which circumstance the bird owes its name.

Sylviorthorhynchus maluroïdes (O. des Murs)

SYLVIORTHORHYNQUE MALUROÏDE.

Garnet-throated Humming-bird

PURPLE-BREASTED CARIB, *Eulampis jugularis* (now Garnet-throated Humming-bird). Hand coloured lithograph by John Gould and Henry C. Richter, pl. 82 from Vol. 2 of John Gould's *A Monograph of the Trochilidae, or Family of Humming-birds*, 1849–61. Size of plate 19″ × 14½″.

First brought to the notice of Europeans during the sixteenth century, Humming-birds are related to Swifts but cannot be mistaken for them as they are probably the most highly specialized and certainly the most diminutive of all birds. Their iridescent plumage and long pointed beaks helped to make them popular objects to collect and at one time they were as familiar as butterflies in the cabinets of the curious. Now they are more popular as living occupants of aviaries.

Some Humming-birds, not always the rarest, are outstandingly beautiful and the Garnet-throated Humming-bird is one. Nearly five inches long, which makes it one of the larger species, it frequents clearings, mountain forests and banana plantations in the Lesser Antilles and is, or at any rate was, common there. One of Gould's favourite Humming-birds, he said of it: 'Nevis is one of the homes of this very beautiful bird; so beautiful indeed is it, that it is an especial favourite with all collectors. It is by no means a rare bird, as is evidenced by the low price at which skins may be purchased; for a few shillings each, the collector may obtain from any of the Parisian dealers as many of the finest examples as he may wish.' Gould also said that the specimens he illustrated in this plate had been sent to the British Museum in 1839 by a Mr T.J. Cottle, who had told Gould that 'it inhabits the high land of the island of Nevis, above the belt of cultivation, and that it never descends to the low ground unless driven down by a hurricane or some other unusual course.'

'I have attempted to represent this bird as accurately as possible,' Gould continues, 'but after all, I find, to my regret, that it conveys only a faint idea of its beauty.' Gould's artistic failure is understandable; the beauty of this Humming-bird, like that of all its close relatives, may not be successfully duplicated by any human art.

EULAMPIS JUGULARIS.

J. Gould and H.C. Richter, del. et lith.

Hullmandel & Walton, Imp.

Fork-tailed Emerald

LONG-TAILED EMERALD, *Chlorostilbon auriceps* (now Fork-tailed Emerald, *Chlorostilbon caniveti*). Hand coloured lithograph, heightened with gold, by J. Gould and H.C. Richter, pl. 67 from Vol. 5 of John Gould's *A Monograph of the Trochilidae, or Family of Humming-birds*, 1849–61. Size of plate 19″ × 14½″.

During the Great Exhibition in London in 1851 one of the more unusual sights was John Gould's collection of Humming-birds. The tiny, gem-like creatures were mounted in a series of glass cases displayed in a building constructed for their reception in the Zoological Gardens. There had never been a show like it before and visitors flocked to see it. Apart from making a handsome profit by charging sixpence a ticket for admission Gould obtained 75 subscribers for his luxurious monograph on the Humming-birds, then in preparation, a complete set of which was priced at £78.15s, making it a costly book in 1851.

This is now regarded as the most outstanding of all Gould's folio bird books. Gould said of it: 'Having from an early period devoted himself to the study of these beautiful birds, and acquired a most valuable and expensive collection of a group peculiar to America and its adjacent islands, the author determined upon publishing a monograph of a family unequalled for the gorgeous and ever-changing brilliancy of their hues, the variety of their form, the singularity of their habits, and the extent of their territorial distribution.'

As in this plate of the Fork-tailed Emerald, based on skins of birds obtained in Mexico, he tried, with some success, to capture the glittering metallic sheen of the Humming-bird's plumage by painting the relevant areas in gold and lightly painting over them with watercolours. Other illustrators before Gould had used gold for this purpose, but he was more successful than most because he used it sparingly and did not try to outdo nature. Of course the wings of a Humming-bird move too rapidly for the human eye to see them as portrayed by Gould, but he made them look very pretty by showing them as if frozen in flight. Indeed, Gould's portrayals of the smallest birds in the world are so decorative that copies of his monograph of them have been broken up and the individual plates framed. Book lovers may demur, but at least this vandalism has made it possible for some of those who cannot afford the five-volume set of Gould's Humming-bird monograph to acquire one or two of the 360 wonderful plates contained in it.

Yellow-cheeked Amazon

DIADEMED AMAZON (now Yellow-cheeked Amazon, *Amazona autumnalis diadema*). Hand coloured lithograph by J. Daverne, pl. 32 from C. de Souancé's *Iconographie des Perroquets*, 1857. Size of plate 21¼" × 13¼".

The gaudy Amazon parrots are amongst the most popular of all cage and aviary birds. Because they also cause extensive damage to fruit trees and grain crops many of them are destroyed annually by farmers, so some of the 26 known species, perhaps including the Yellow-cheeked Amazon, are in danger of extinction.

One of the outstanding nineteenth-century books about parrots, Charles de Souancé's *Iconographie des Perroquets* contains many beautiful illustrations. This one is unusually charming for its time because it shows the bird in a natural and – to parrot lovers – a familiar pose, although its perch is the artist's conventional truncated branch. One of the four well-defined forms of the Yellow-cheeked Amazon, it comes from the forests of north-western Brazil. Judging by the lifelike pose of the one shown in this illustration it was almost certainly seen alive by the artist, about the middle of the last century. The accompanying text also states that, although it is a large species, it lives amicably with smaller, weaker parrots, a rare quality in this family. It has been exhibited at the London Zoo but does not seem to have been bred successfully there or elsewhere in Europe in recent years.

J. Daverne, del et lith.   P. Bertrand Editeur.   Lith. Juhet à Tours.

Chrysotis diadema (Spix)

Society Islands Pigeon

SOCIETY ISLANDS PIGEON, *Carpophaga aurorae* (now *Ducula aurorae*). Hand coloured engraving by Titian R. Peale, pl. 24 from the *Atlas* to J. Cassin's *Ornithology of the United States Exploring Expedition*, 1858. Size of plate 16½ × 11″.

This is one of the larger and heavier fruit-eating pigeons of the world, collectively known as imperial pigeons. It is about sixteen inches in length and is very conspicuously coloured. Peale, who described it as new to science, wrote of it, 'This beautiful Pigeon was found in great abundance in high woody districts amongst the coral rocks on Aurora or Maitea Island, and of the Society Group . . . they were not shy, but it was difficult to see them when sitting in the thick foliage, as they remained perfectly still on our approach . . . This bird may be regarded as one of the most interesting discoveries of the Expedition and is one of the most handsome as well as one of the largest species of the family of Pigeons.'

Because of continuous human persecution since the beginning of the twentieth century the Society Islands Pigeon is now probably extinct in Tahiti (only ten could be counted there in 1972). On the island of Makatea (or Aurora) in the Tuamotu Archipelago, on the other hand, it is increasing in numbers now that phosphate mining has ceased. Sadly, the day is unlikely to arrive when it will be seen again 'in great abundance' as it was by Titian Rembrandt Peale, its western discoverer.

Carpophaga auroræ. Peale.

T.R.Peale del.

W.H.Dougal sc.

Perouse's Fruit Dove

PEROUSE'S FRUIT DOVE, *Ptilonopus perousii*. Hand coloured engraving by Titian R. Peale, pl. 33 from the *Atlas* to J. Cassin's *Ornithology of the United States Exploring Expedition*, 1858. Size of plate 16½″ × 11″.

This very attractive pigeon, measuring about ten inches in length, was first obtained in the Fiji group of islands during the voyage of the United States Exploring Expedition led by Charles Wilkes between 1838 and 1842. The ornithologist on the expedition was Titian Rembrandt Peale (with a name like that he just had to be an artist too) who drew and engraved this plate.

Peale said of the bird, 'This is one of the most delicately colored and gracefully formed of the entire family of Pigeons . . . It is, perhaps, the most beautiful bird discovered in the course of the voyage of the Expedition.' It occurs in Samoa as well as the Fiji group but has become very scarce.

Ptilonopus Perousei. Peale.

Th. Peale del.

Rawdon sc.

Quetzal

QUETZAL, *Pharomachrus mocinno*. Hand coloured lithograph by John Gould and William Hart, pl. 1 from Gould's *A Monograph of the Trogonidae* (2nd edition), 1858–75. Size of plate 20½″ × 13¾″.

This is a remarkable picture of one of the world's most remarkable birds. It is the most resplendent of the Trogons, a family of birds which frequents the densest and darkest parts of tropical forests. The Quetzal's body is no bigger than that of a domestic pigeon, but its enormously long tail accounts for three-quarters of its total length of about four feet. This created a problem for Gould who tried to represent birds at their natural size, but he solved it by showing the tail feathers of the male bird curving up and over its back. Normally, as the other two males in the picture show, the tail would hang downwards. The male is also brilliantly coloured, with carmine on the underparts, contrasting black feathers around the eyes and iridescent, greenish-gold plumage elsewhere – a lovely sight.

An inhabitant of rainforests in mountainous regions from southern Mexico to Nicaragua, it is natural that the Quetzal should have become a bird sacred to the Aztecs and the Maya, the ancient chiefs wearing tail plumes plucked from living birds. Although its tail feathers – the obvious reason for its elevated status – could be removed for the decoration of a privileged few, killing it was forbidden. In Central America there is the belief that a captured Quetzal dies of a broken heart (indeed it does soon die in captivity) and the bird has now become a symbol of freedom. It is also the national bird of Guatemala.

PHAROMACRUS MOCINNO.

Knysna Touraco

KNYSNA TOURACO, *Musophaga persa* (now *Tauraco corythaix*). Hand coloured lithograph by P.W.M. Trap after a drawing by Herman Schlegel, pl. 9 from Schlegel's *De Toerako's afgebeeld en beschreven*, 1860. Size of plate 25½″ × 20″.

The plates in Schlegel's book are well composed, delicately coloured and very large. Each occupies a surface area almost as large as an Audubon plate. As the Touracos range in size from 15 to 25 inches they scarcely deserve such lavish treatment, but the author had already published a treatise on falconry which had been highly praised for the splendid and extravagantly large plates (by Joseph Wolf) which illustrated it. Perhaps Schlegel, who drew the Touracos himself, hoped that his subjects would look more impressive on large plates.

Touracos are found over much of Africa. Most of them spend their lives deep in forests where their bright colours are minimized. They eat plantains, fruits and insects and are able to run along branches in the manner of squirrels. The rich red colour which is such a striking feature of some of them is imparted by a pigment called turacin. If a red feather from a Touraco is agitated in a glass of water the pigment will dye the water pink. Fortunately for the bird the pigment does not seem to be washed out of its plumage by the tropical rains.

Blue Plantain-eater

BLUE PLANTAIN-EATER, *Musophaga gigantea* (now *Corythaeola cristata*). Hand coloured lithograph by P.W.M. Trap after a drawing by Hermann Schlegel, pl. 12 from Schlegel's *De Toerako's afgebeeld en beschreven*, 1860. Size of plate 25½″ × 20″.

Hermann Schlegel, who became Director of the Leiden Natural History Museum, wrote and sometimes illustrated several books about various aspects of the animal kingdom. He became a leading authority on birds and his book on the Touracos is an outstanding contribution to the ornithology of West Africa, not least because of the large size of its plates. But the Blue Plantain-eater, the giant of the family, was too large to be portrayed at its full length of 30 inches.

This bird is widespread in West Africa and is sometimes locally abundant. It runs and hops along branches in the tops of trees, a conspicuous creature with its blue plumage, long black-tipped tail and distinctive black crest. It may often be seen eating the fruit of the umbrella tree, is often noisy, and builds a platform of twigs in a treetop as a nest for its two greenish-blue eggs. It is refreshing to know that such a large and attractive bird as this has not been persecuted to the point of extinction.

Gyrfalcon

GREENLAND FALCON, *Falco candicans* (now Gyrfalcon, *Falco rusticolus*). Hand coloured lithograph by Joseph Wolf and Henry Constantine Richter, pl. 13 from Vol. 1 of John Gould's *The Birds of Great Britain*, 1862–73. Size of plate 19″ × 14″.

This is not just another bird picture; it is a masterpiece. At once dramatic, sensitive, balanced and completely satisfying, it could only have been produced by someone profoundly knowledgeable about his subject, someone who could use his imagination intelligently to achieve a masterly composition. It is the work of Joseph Wolf at his superlative best.

For a while after Wolf came to England from his native Germany in 1848 he discovered that naturalists were interested only in scientific correctness; they mistrusted artistic drawings. But his lifelike portraits of birds and other animals soon won them over and he could please himself which commissions he chose to take up. Even the redoubtable John Gould found it difficult to get bird drawings out of him; but when he did so the results could be stunning, especially when he obtained some watercolours of birds of prey, subjects which Wolf had made peculiarly his own. The published lithographs of these and other wildlife subjects brought him great respect, not only in England but also in Europe and North America.

Wolf had scant respect for many of Gould's published bird portraits, which he considered tame and lacking in vitality, but Gould's admiration for Wolf's artistry was unrestrained. Wolf was a fine ornithologist as well as an artist and he had made a close study of many of his subjects. Gould had first-hand proof of this when he accompanied Wolf to Norway in the summer of 1856. While Gould exhibited his skill at preparing the specimens shot by both of them Wolf showed him how to discover a Red-throated Bluebreast's nest by recognizing its song. But Wolf's abiding legacy is his series of portraits of birds of prey, among which this study of the Gyrfalcon is pre-eminent.

13.

FALCO CANDICANS, *J. F. Gmel.*

J. Wolf & H.C. Richter, del et lith.

Greenland Falcon. light race. adult and young

Walter Imp.

Snowy Owl

SNOWY OWL, *Nyctea nivea* (now *Nyctea scandiniaca*). Hand coloured litho-graph by Henry C. Richter after a drawing by Joseph Wolf, pl. 34 from Vol. 1 of John Gould's *The Birds of Great Britain*, 1862–73. Size of plate 21½″ × 14½″.

It is a moot point who was the more accomplished illustrator of owls, Edward Lear or Joseph Wolf. The high point of Lear's career as a bird artist had been reached by the time he was 25, at which age Wolf still had many productive years ahead of him. Wolf was also the better field ornithologist and his eyesight was superior. Brilliant though Lear's studies of owls may be, they lack the total truth that is in those done by Wolf. It would be difficult for anyone to improve upon this study by Wolf of a Snowy Owl, for example, even though the polar bears seen in the background could have been left out. The bird is shown close to the viewer against a backdrop of a distant landscape seen from a height, a favourite device of Wolf's, making the bird seem formidably large (as it attains a length of 26 inches, about twice the size of a Barn Owl, it really is large). Wolf's bird is a female, the male bird being less conspicuously banded and barred.

The eyes of this handsome bird are remarkably large in relation to the size of its head and they enable it to see well in the dark. Nevertheless, it does most of its hunting by day, feeding on lemmings and other rodents, rabbits and birds as large as the Ptarmigan. A bird of the Artic tundra, the Snowy Owl is sometimes seen as far south as Scotland, but to see one anywhere in the wild is a rare privilege.

34.

NYCTEA NIVEA.

J.Wolf and H.C.Richter del. et lith.

Walter & Cohn Imp.

Robin

<small>ROBIN OR REDBREAST, *Erythacus rubecula*. Hand coloured lithograph by Henry C. Richter, pl. 48 from Vol. 2 of John Gould's *The Birds of Great Britain*, 1862–73. Size of plate 21½″ × 14″.</small>

More often than most authors of illustrated books about birds John Gould had to learn how best to fill a large piece of paper with studies of small birds. He solved the problem magnificently in his multi-volume monograph of the Humming-birds, usually by showing several of the tiny creatures together, some of them frozen in flight and hovering over exotic plants. The more subdued colouring of the small British birds and their more retiring ways, however, called for a different approach.

In this plate Gould's artist Henry Constantine Richter has made clever use of cascading green leaves of ivy to show off the complementary colour of the Robins' breasts. At the same time he has filled the folio page with a very attractive, if sentimental composition. The apparently precarious state of the young birds in their nest adds a little unintentional drama.

In Britain, where it is considered the national bird, the Robin has a close and trusting relationship with humans, as any gardener will confirm. In Europe it is usually a shy bird. To Richter it was a red bird, the European equivalent, perhaps, of the Common Cardinal of North America which Mark Catesby illustrated in a similar, if more primitive manner, in his much earlier book *The Natural History of Carolina, Florida and the Bahama Islands* (see Plate 2).

48.

ERYTHACUS RUBECULA.

J. Gould & H.C. Richter, del. et lith.

Walter, Imp.

Gannet

GANNET, *Sulu bassana*. Hand coloured lithograph by Joseph Wolf and Henry C. Richter, pl. 54 from Vol. 5 of John Gould's *The Birds of Great Britain*, 1862–73. Size of plate 21½″ × 14½″.

A large bird, some 36 inches long when mature, the Gannet takes three years to acquire its adult plumage. Although it breeds on land it is strictly a sea bird – it even sleeps on the water – and lives entirely on fish, gliding for hours over the sea looking for them. When it finds a shoal it is usually joined by its fellows, then it dives down like a stone, its wings closed, and splashes noisily into the water, emerging a few moments later to throw back its head and gobble down its prey.

Gannets are found mostly on islands with steep cliffs off Iceland, the Faroes, the British Isles, Channel Islands, Brittany, the Gulf of St Lawrence and off Newfoundland. They are particularly abundant around the British Isles and constitute the most noteworthy feature of the Bass Rock, where they normally arrive in about the middle of February or the beginning of March. There, as elsewhere, they nest colonially in every available spot, laying a single egg in a shallow nest consisting mostly of seaweed. The noise made by such a colony may be heard a mile away. Most of the birds depart in October but year after year they return to the same site to breed. The Gannet's incredible rapacity is suggested in Wolf's evocative study, even though it shows the bird at rest.

SULA BASSANA, *Linn.*

J.Wolf & H.C.Richter, del. et lith.

Walter, Imp.

Common Paradise Kingfisher

MORTY ISLAND KINGFISHER, *Tanysiptera doris* (now Common Paradise King-fisher, *Tanysiptera galatea doris*). Hand coloured lithograph by John Gerrard Keulemans, pl. 101 from R. Bowdler Sharpe's *A Monograph of the Alcedinidae; or Family of Kingfishers*, 1868–71. Size of plate 11½″ × 8½″.

There are many different kinds of Kingfisher in the world, including some which make the Common Kingfisher of European countries look very insignificant. But even though some of the exotic species are larger and more resplendent they are still obviously Kingfishers, especially about the head and beak. Perhaps the most elegant and beautiful of all the Kingfishers are those with long tails ending in rackets (they are called Racket-tailed Kingfishers in consequence) which live in the Moluccas, northern Australia and New Guinea.

It was from a skin obtained at Morotai Island in the Moluccas, in the collection of the great traveller–naturalist Alfred Russell Wallace, that Keulemans drew the adult depicted in this plate. Wallace, who had observed related Kingfishers in dense forests during his eastern travels, told Bowdler Sharpe: 'They rest on branches three to five feet from the ground, and dart down on their prey, often with such force as to stick their bill into the ground.' They are known to feed on insects, land snails and other small invertebrates.

TANYSIPTERA DORIS.

Torrent Duck

TORRENT DUCK, *Merganetta turneri* (now *Merganetta armata turneri*). Hand coloured lithograph by Joseph Smit, pl. C from Philip L. Sclater and Osbert Salvin's *Exotic Ornithology*, 1869. Size of plate 14″ × 10″.

Very little is known about this bird, one of the half-a-dozen or so races of the Torrent Duck. The specimen illustrated in the foreground is a male, one of a pair which belonged to a Mr Whitely who brought it to England in a collection of birds he had made at Tinta, a village situated about 11,000 feet up in the Andes of southern Peru, not far from the ancient city of Cuzco.

Measuring about seventeen inches in length the Torrent Duck lives along rapid mountain streams, makes its nest in holes in the banks, and is an excellent swimmer and diver. It is doubtful that the placid setting of Joseph Smit's picture has much in common with the actual conditions encountered by the Torrent Duck, but then Smit had never seen a mountain stream high up in the Andes. He had been paid to provide a convincing portrait of a supposedly undescribed duck and in this endeavour he was tolerably successful.

MERGANETTA TURNERI

Golden Pheasant

GOLDEN PHEASANT, *Thaumalea picta* (now *Chrysolopus pictus*). Hand coloured lithograph by Joseph Wolf and Joseph Smit, pl. 15 from Vol. 2 of Daniel Giraud Elliot's *A Monograph of the Phasianidae, or Family of the Pheasants*, 1872. Size of plate 23½" × 18".

If Joseph Wolf is one of the acknowledged masters of bird art his mastery of that art is nowhere more evident than in some of his illustrations to Daniel Giraud Elliot's impressive monograph of the Pheasants. This exquisite study of the Golden Pheasant is proof enough that Wolf could draw game birds as well as he drew birds of prey. Some of the credit for this and the other plates in the book should go to Joseph Smit, the lithographer, who served Wolf and Elliot well.

The Golden Pheasant is a native of central and north-western China. Rare above 6,500 feet, it avoids dense forests and is well adapted to a life among the rocky mountain ridges which constitute its natural habitat. The cock bird, with a total length of about 42 inches and a tail length of about 30 inches, is much larger in all respects than the hen and is surely one of the most gorgeous of all birds. Elliot's accompanying text describes the bird well: 'One of the longest-known species of Pheasants, the present bird retains its position as one of the most beautiful. Early introduced into Europe from China, its native country, it is familiar to everyone; and no bird is more suited, both as regards its gentle disposition and strong contrasting colours of plumage, to become an inhabitant of the aviary . . . The male of this beautiful species has the top of the head and occiput covered with a long silky amber-coloured crest – an extensive ruff, springing from the back of the head, hiding the neck. The features of these ornamental appendages are deep orange-red, with a dark blue bar at the tip, and can be spread out and brought over the face at will.'

Were it rarer, the Golden Pheasant would be popularly accounted one of the wonders of the natural world – or, more likely, it would now be extinct. Beauty, a tolerance of captivity and an amiable disposition have ensured its survival.

J. Wolf & J. Smit, del. & lith.

M & N Hanhart, imp.

THAUMALEA PICTA

Red Jungle-fowl

RED JUNGLE-FOWL, *Gallus ferrugineus* (now *Gallus gallus*). Hand coloured lithograph by Joseph Wolf and Joseph Smit, pl. 32 from Vol. 2 of Daniel Giraud Elliot's *A Monograph of the Phasianidae, or Family of the Pheasants*, 1872. Size of plate 23½″ × 18″.

In spite of the comb and wattles about its head this bird is a pheasant. Seemingly out of place in a book illustrating the world's pheasants, the Red Jungle-fowl would also seem out of place in a book about the world's domestic fowl, even though all the many existing forms are descended from birds similar to it. The fighting cocks of today resemble the Red Jungle-fowl much closer than do any of our domestic hens and chickens. It may have been an addiction to the sport of cockfighting among primitive people that led to the early spread and domestication of the Red Jungle-fowl.

In its wild form, however, this bird has a kind of regal bearing which is well captured in this fine drawing. It is as if Joseph Wolf had wanted to make the bird worthy of its place in one of the finest bird books ever published. Fittingly Elliot dedicated his monograph to Wolf, 'whose unrivalled talent has graced this work with its chief attraction and whose marvellous power of delineating animal life renders him unequalled in our time'.

GALLUS FERRUGINEUS.

Chestnut-breasted Coronet

CHESTNUT-BREASTED CORONET, *Clytolaema matthewsi* (now *Boissoneaua matthewsi*). Hand coloured lithograph by L. Bevalet, unnumbered plate from Vol. 2 of E. Mulsant and E. Verraux's *Histoire Naturelle des Oiseaux-Mouches, ou Colibris, constituant la Famille des Trochilidés*, 1874–77. Size of plate 12½" × 9½".

It is so natural to associate Humming-birds with the folio-sized illustrations of them published by John Gould that it is easy to overlook the many illustrations of these exquisite little birds which were published in other, less opulent publications during the nineteenth century. French naturalists had always taken a special interest in Humming-birds and the plate reproduced here comes from a substantial monograph published several years after Gould's, the *Histoire Naturelle des Oiseaux-Mouches* of Mulsant and Verraux.

Less grand and less realistic than a Gould plate, it still captures the ephemeral and delicate nature of the bird, reflecting the miniaturist tradition of French natural history art. An imaginative jeweller could have been well satisfied if he had created a piece resembling this picture of the Chestnut-breasted Coronet resting on a *Poinciana*.

Credit for its discovery in Peru must go to Mr Matthews, a little-known ornithologist, after whom it was named and by whom many other discoveries in natural history were made. Under the description of this bird in John Gould's monograph of the Humming-birds we learn that 'the life of its discoverer fell a victim to the pestiferous region in which it was found'. Even minor discoveries such as this may exact a high price from their discoverer.

CLYTOLAEMA MATTHEWSI.

(*Poinciana pulcherrima*)

Crossbill

CROSSBILL, *Loxia curvirostris*. Hand coloured lithograph by Edward Neale, unnumbered plate from Vol. 1 of E.T. Booth's *Rough Notes on the Birds Observed during Twenty-five Years' Shooting and Collecting in the British Islands*, 1881–87. Size of plate 16½″ × 13″.

Edward Thomas Booth, a wealthy man, travelled all over Britain looking for birds to shoot and to add to his museum. He taught himself taxidermy and set up all his birds in glass cases: most of them are now housed in the Brighton Museum. Edward Neale, an artist noted for his ability to draw fledglings, provided all the drawings for Booth's idiosyncratic book. In some of the illustrations the birds look as though drawn from stuffed specimens – which they were – but others have more vitality.

'The Crossbill is soon reconciled to confinement,' said Booth, 'and becomes a most amusing cage-bird. I had many opportunities of watching a fine male in the possession of a keeper near Inverness. This bird, which was captured in a somewhat singular manner (having been knocked down from a tree by a fir-cone which was flung at him) was in the red plumage when taken, but eventually moulted to a dull green.' About the two different stages of plumage exhibited by the male Crossbills in Neale's lithograph he had this to say: 'The principal figure is taken from an adult in the full breeding plumage obtained in the spring. The bird with a tinge of orange on the feathers is probably immature. This specimen was shot on July 6, 1876.' Crossbills use their crossed mandibles to extract seeds from the cones of larch, pine, spruce and other conifers.

CROSSBILL.

MALE ADULT & MALE IMMATURE.

Hawaiian Goose

HAWAIIAN GOOSE, *Bernicla sandvicensis* (now *Branta sandvicensis*). Hand coloured lithograph by Frederick William Frohawk, pl. opposite p. 150 from S.B. Wilson and A.H. Evans' *Aves Hawaiiensis: the Birds of the Sandwich Islands*, 1890–99. Size of plate 12½″ × 9½″.

The Cambridge ornithologists S.B. Wilson and A.H. Evans made two voyages to the Hawaiian Islands and Frohawk provided all the hand coloured lithographs for the book they wrote about the birds they studied there. The authors took ten years to complete their book so Frohawk had plenty of time to produce his illustrations for it; the lithograph of the Hawaiian Goose is an example of his work at its best.

This attractive bird, which attains a length of about 24 inches, is found on Hawaii and on the island of Maui. It has had a chequered history. At one time it was common, but when Wilson and Evans went in search of it at the end of the nineteenth century it was confined to one district of the island of Hawaii. Its favourite breeding haunts were at an altitude of between 5,000 and 7,000 feet on the grass-covered lava-flows at Kona, as unsuitable a place for a duck to breed as can be imagined. Wilson and Evans said that it was 'clearly doomed to extinction before many years are past'. Their gloomy prophecy was nearly fulfilled; in 1947 there were only about fifty birds living in the wild. Then the late Sir Peter Scott's Wildfowl Trust in England and the Hawaiian Board of Agriculture came to the rescue and, about 30 years later, there were probably at least 600 birds existing in the wild.

It does not help a bird's chances of survival if, like the Hawaiian Goose, it is good to eat; its flesh is said to make an excellent soup. Fortunately it soon becomes tame, which helps it flourish in captivity.

F.W.Frohawk del. et lith.

West, Newman imp

BERNICLA SANDVICENSIS

Blue Bird of Paradise

PRINCE RUDOLPH'S BIRD OF PARADISE, *Paradisornis rudolphii* (now Blue Bird of Paradise, *Paradisaea rudolphi*). Hand coloured lithograph by William Hart, pl. 29 from Vol. 1 of R. Bowdler Sharpe's *Monograph of the Paradiseidae, or Birds of Paradise, and Ptilorhynchidae, or Bower-birds*, 1891–98. Size of plate 22″ × 14″.

When Alfred Russell Wallace, the English traveller–naturalist, returned to England from the Indonesian archipelago in 1862 he brought with him the first two Birds of Paradise to reach the western world alive. They were a sensation. Something of the excitement which such birds inspired in ornithologists during the second half of the nineteenth century is conveyed in Richard Bowdler Sharpe's text accompanying the lovely illustration reproduced here: 'This wonderful bird is an inhabitant of south-eastern New Guinea, and it is not saying too much to state that among all the extraordinary birds which inhabit the earth, this is one of the most striking. Accustomed as naturalists have been to the fantastic coloration of the Birds of Paradise, with their long flowing yellow or red plumes, no one could have expected that a bird existed which had blue streamers, as we find to be the case in the present bird.'

German and Austrian collectors and ornithologists were actively interested in the remarkable fauna and flora of New Guinea in the 1880s and this was one of their most outstanding discoveries. Otto Finsch, an Austrian ornithologist, named the bird after the Archduke Rudolph of Hapsburg (and he also commemorated Rudolph's Belgian consort by describing Princess Stephanie's Bird of Paradise as new to science).

In those days bird artists often had to overcome considerable difficulties when illustrating rare birds. The figure of the adult male in this illustration, for example, was taken from a drawing made by John Gerrard Keulemans from the specimen described originally by Finsch in the Dresden Museum; the lower figure was drawn from a preserved specimen in the Natural History Museum in London. It is difficult to believe that Hart had never seen a living example of this lovely bird.

PARADISORNIS RUDOLPHI, *Finsch.*

W. Hart del. et lith.

Mintern Bros. imp.

Raggiana Bird of Paradise

RED-PLUMED BIRD OF PARADISE, *Paradisea raggiana* (now Raggiana Bird of Paradise, *Paradisaea raggiana*). Hand coloured lithograph by W. M. Hart, pl. 21 from Vol. 1 of R. Bowdler Sharpe's *Monograph of the Paradiseidae, or Birds of Paradise, and Ptilorhynchidae, or Bower-birds*, 1891–98. Size of plate 21½″ × 14″.

In 1522, when the prepared skins of two gaudy birds were brought back to Spain from the Molucca Islands on board Magellan's ship, the *Victoria*, they were looked upon as visitors from paradise; and similar birds have been known as Birds of Paradise ever since. For many years specimens reached Europe minus their legs and feet (they had been inexpertly prepared by native taxidermists) which is how Linnaeus came to describe one of the commoner species as 'the footless paradise bird, *Paradisea apoda*'. Some of these footless birds may be seen flying through the skies of oil paintings by some of the old masters.

Many different species live in the great island of New Guinea, one of them the Raggiana Bird of Paradise. Because the filmy plumes of this and some other species may be lifted up and raised over the back in a fountain-like display the birds look larger than they are; and in some book illustrations they may look much larger. The bodies of the largest species are no longer than crows. By contrast the length of the smallest known species, the King Bird of Paradise, is a mere six inches, including its tail feathers. The total length of the Red-plumed Bird of Paradise is about eighteen inches. An inquisitive bird, it often approaches to within a few yards of its pursuer, stays motionless for a few seconds watching him, then stretches out its neck, flaps its wings, and utters a strange cry, which usually brings other individuals of the same species out from cover to join it. The flesh is as tough as leather even after having been boiled for hours.

William Matthew Hart, one of John Gould's most gifted artists, painted many of the original watercolours for Bowdler Sharpe's impressive monograph. It is difficult to understand how Hart, based in London and with only prepared skins to work from, could paint lifelike pictures of exotic birds such as these and could place them in realistic and convincing settings. Even with the help of sophisticated camera equipment it would be difficult to achieve better results.

W. Hart del. et lith.

PARADISEA RAGGIANA, Sclater.

Mintern Bros. imp.

Blue-bellied Roller

BLUE-BELLIED ROLLER, *Coracias cyanogaster*. Hand coloured lithograph by John Gerrard Keulemans, pl. 12 from H.E. Dresser's *A Monograph of the Coraciidae, or the Family of the Rollers*, 1893. Size of plate 15″ × 11½″.

This is one of about seventeen species of birds collectively known as Rollers, of which about a dozen may be considered truly worthy of the name (which is derived from their acrobatic 'rolling' performances in the air, performances made the more spectacular by the lovely colours revealed when they spread their wings and tail feathers). Most of them live in Africa south of the Sahara while four species range eastwards to northern Australia and the Solomon group.

A solitary Roller is often seen sitting on an exposed branch waiting for the chance to seize an insect, a small rodent, a frog or a lizard, but many Rollers congregate from over a wide area to enjoy an aerial feast in company when flying ants or locusts are swarming. They usually nest in holes in trees but some species will excavate a hollow in tree-termite nests; two to four rounded whitish eggs make up the normal clutch.

The Blue-bellied Roller, which occurs from Senegal to Zaire and the Sudan, was originally described in 1806 by the French naturalist Levaillant as 'le Rollier à ventre bleu', suggesting that its 'rolling' activities were known at that time. The English-speaking residents of India and Africa often call them 'Blue Jays'; in some respects Rollers do look like Jays but they are unrelated. As usual, Keulemans has represented the bird in profile. This shows its essential features but only hints at the gorgeous colours it reveals when rolling in the air.

BLUEBELLIED ROLLER.
CORACIAS CYANOGASTER.

Hanhart imp.

Hawaii O'O

HAWAII O'O, *Moho nobilis*. Hand coloured lithograph by John Gerrard Keulemans, pl. 72 from W. Rothschild's *The Avifauna of Laysan and the Neighbouring Islands*, 1893–1900. Size of plate 14½″ × 10½″.

When the Hon. Walter Rothschild wrote about the Hawaii O'O at the close of the nineteenth century it was still a fairly common, if shy and elusive bird. Hunters are known to have bagged a thousand specimens in 1898, for instance, in woods at Wailuku, Hawaii. But since 1934, when one was heard singing on the slopes of Mauna Loa, it seems to have become extinct. The wonder is that it did not disappear much earlier; it was destined long ago to be hunted to extinction for the sake of its lovely yellow feathers.

Some of those who took part in Captain Cook's third voyage of discovery in the late 1770s acquired many curios from the inhabitants of the Hawaiian Islands. These included some beautiful cloaks and other garments made principally from the feathers of certain native birds, including the O'O, several of them having been formerly worn by male members of the ruling classes. The cloak of an exalted chief could contain more than half a million feathers of various kinds; it required hundreds or even thousands of O'O birds to provide sufficient yellow feathers for a single cloak.

The Hon. Walter Rothschild was, indirectly, one of many who helped to kill off the O'O. A keen collector of birds who could afford to pay well for specimens, he tells us in the text accompanying this coloured plate that the artist had worked from skins in his museum at Tring. Like so many exotic creatures this bird was just too beautiful to be allowed to survive. But Rothschild had also ensured that its beauty could be appreciated by posterity. The picture he commissioned from Keulemans will remain the best known likeness of the Hawaii O'O for many years to come.

J.G.Keulemans del.et lith.

MOHO NOBILIS, (MERREM) ♂ & ♀ AD.

Mintern. Bros. imp.

Great Auk

Great Auk, *Alca impennis*. Chromolithograph, from an article, *Der Riese-nalk, Alca impennis* L., by Wilhelm Blasius in J.F. Naumann's *Naturgeschichte der Vogel Mitteleuropas*, 1895–1905. Size of plate 15¼″ × 11″.

Like the Dodo, the appearance of a living Great Auk is conjectural, for a living specimen of this flightless bird has not been seen since 1844, when a breeding pair was clubbed to death on an island off the coast of Iceland. Apart from the evidence of mounted and unmounted skins in museums and private collections our knowledge of its probable appearance in life must be obtained from eye-witness descriptions and mostly inadequate illustrations . Nineteeth-century illustrations of the Great Auk, including the one repro-duced here, were therefore mostly products of scientific deduction, artistic imagination and guesswork. This illustration, published in 1903, shows both male and female birds in a naturalistic setting and is as convincing as any that have been attempted.

Originally the Greak Auk was known to European sailors as the 'Pen-guin', a word possibly derived from the Welsh language (*pen* = head, *gwyn* = white). Later, when sailors and explorers encountered the black and white seabirds of the seas around Antarctica the name 'Penguin' was mistakenly transferred to them. How curious it is that the original name given to the long-extinct Great Auk, a bird of northern seas, has been appropriated for a dozen or more different species of equally flightless birds from southern seas! With any luck these southern birds will not suffer the same fate as their northern counterparts.

One-wattled Cassowary

ONE-WATTLED CASSOWARY, *Casuarius unappendiculatus*. Hand coloured lithograph by John Gerrard Keulemans, pl. 30 from Walter Rothschild's *Monograph of the Genus Casuarius*, 1900. Size of plate 12½″ × 9½″.

Walter Rothschild, the eccentric and wealthy son of the first Lord Rothschild, created a private museum of natural history at Tring and assembled in it a large and valuable collection of birds and bird skins. He also published several treatises on birds, including one on the Cassowaries, illustrated by Keulemans, that tireless illustrator of countless perching birds: he must have found it a pleasant change to draw birds almost as tall as himself and which habitually stood on the ground. The bird illustrated here, which gets its name from the single wattle hanging from in front of its neck, is about five feet six inches tall when walking but a towering six feet eight inches when upright.

Many different kinds of Cassowary have been described, all from New Guinea, northern Australia and adjacent islands, but ornithologists now consider that there are only three species, each with several subspecies. Unusually among birds the females are larger than the males. Apart from the brightly coloured skin on the head and neck the most distinctive feature of a Cassowary is the bony helmet or casque on the top of its head, which it uses to brush aside obstructions in its path. Unlike the Ostrich it does not have tail feathers.

Cassowaries are very bad-tempered and make formidable opponents, their strong, sharp claws being capable of ripping open humans rash enough to confront them. They have often slashed and seriously injured zoo keepers; even rats and mice are speedily trampled to death by captive Cassowaries. As they are said to be able to run at speeds of up to 30 miles an hour the only way to escape from them in forests is to take to the trees. The One-wattled Cassowary puts up its feathers when angry and emits a peculiar blowing cry followed by a pig-like grunting. This bird emphatically does not make a good pet.

J.G.Keulemans del. et lith.

3/5

Mintern Bros. imp.

CASUARIUS UNIAPPENDICULATUS.

Common Partridge

COMMON PARTRIDGE, *Perdix perdix*. Limited edition print of 'Summer Partridges', after an original painting by Archibald Thorburn, dated 1926, the Tryon Gallery, London. Size of plate 18″ × 13″.

Archibald Thorburn's best work as a bird artist was accomplished during the first thirty years of the twentieth century. Famous in his lifetime for his sensitive portrayals of young birds, game birds and birds of prey he may be seen now as a natural successor to the great Joseph Wolf. His fame was such that he found a profitable market in the production of limited edition prints each of which he signed. Printed on superior paper and framed, these prints are as popular now as when they were first issued. 'Summer Partridges' is a good example of Thorburn's work in this genre.

Our first sight of a Partridge is often of a rotund, reddish-brown bird running away from us and then whirring into flight, gliding to the ground again shortly afterwards to resume its running before coming to a stop. Typically a bird of agricultural land, especially in corn-growing districts, it eats grain, plants and insects. Sometimes it may be seen at roadsides pecking for grit or enjoying a dust bath.

Well seen in this picture is the large grown patch on the lower part of the breast which distinguishes it from other Partridges. This patch and the markings on the head of the cock bird are more conspicuous and brighter than those of the hen. This is not only the most widespread European Partridge but it is the only Partridge found in central and northern Europe.

Kestrel

KESTREL, *Falco tinnunculus*. Original oil painting by George Lodge in the Tryon Gallery, London. Size of painting 18″ × 13″.

George Lodge's portraits of predatory birds are widely regarded by those most qualified to know as being among the finest ever painted. A prolific artist, a great deal of his work has appeared as book illustrations. But why, it may be asked, include an oil painting in a book otherwise devoted to prints? The answer is simple. Many of the Lodge illustrations in bird books by the late David Bannerman and others are themselves printed reproductions of oil paintings. They have become prints merely by being reproduced on paper. In the same way Lodge's painting of a pair of Kestrels has now been reproduced by a photomechanical process to provide multiple copies of a print. A new print has been created!

The most striking feature of the Kestrel is the way it hovers, but keen bird watchers will have recognised it perching on trees, buildings, rocks and overhead wires. Often it selects a post or similar vantage point from which it will swoop down on its prey which comprises small mammals, small birds, insects and worms.

The female Kestrel is less strikingly marked than the male, being mostly reddish-brown. The combination of blue-grey and brownish colours displayed by the male is unique among the smaller predatory birds of Europe.

Unfortunately this bird, which is not an agricultural pest, has suffered from the effects of pesticides. At the same time it has incurred the wrath of game-keepers who destroy it as ruthlessly as it destroys chicks of the Grouse and the Partridge. But it is still the most familiar of European predatory birds.

INDEX